Interdisciplinarity

American University Studies

Series V
Philosophy

Vol. 187

PETER LANG
New York • Washington, D.C./Baltimore • Boston • Bern
Frankfurt am Main • Berlin • Brussels • Vienna • Oxford

Michael Finkenthal

Interdisciplinarity

Toward the Definition of a Metadiscipline?

PETER LANG
New York • Washington, D.C./Baltimore • Boston • Bern
Frankfurt am Main • Berlin • Brussels • Vienna • Oxford

Library of Congress Cataloging-in-Publication Data

Finkenthal, Michael.
Interdisciplinarity: toward the definition
of a metadiscipline? / Michael Finkenthal.
p. cm. — (American university studies. Series V, Philosophy; vol. 187)
Includes bibliographical references.
1. Interdisciplinary approach to knowledge. I. Title. II. Series.
BD255 .F56   001—dc21   00-056777
ISBN 0-8204-4078-7
ISSN 0739-6392

Die Deutsche Bibliothek-CIP-Einheitsaufnahme

Finkenthal, Michael:
Interdisciplinarity: toward the definition
of a metadiscipline? / Michael Finkenthal.
–New York; Washington, D.C./Baltimore; Boston; Bern;
Frankfurt am Main; Berlin; Brussels; Vienna; Oxford: Lang.
(American university studies: Ser. 5, Philosophy; Vol. 187)
ISBN 0-8204-4078-7

© 2001 Peter Lang Publishing, Inc., New York

All rights reserved.
Reprint or reproduction, even partially, in all forms such as microfilm,
xerography, microfiche, microcard, and offset strictly prohibited.

Socrates:...anyone who leaves behind him a written manual, and likewise anyone who takes it over from him, on the supposition that such writing will provide something reliable and permanent, must be exceedingly simple-minded.

Plato, *Phaedrus*

To my wife, Monica, who made writing this book possible

Contents

Preface xi

1. Introduction 1
2. The Greek Way to Disciplinarian Thinking 15
3. Western Thinking between the End of the Greek World and the Middle Ages 29
4. The Turning Point 43
5. Why Did the Far East Not Have Its Scientific Revolution? 61
6. Disciplinarian Thinking 71
7. Interdisciplinarity, Old and New 79
8. The Issue of "Two Cultures" Revisited 95
9. Disciplinarity, Interdisciplinarity, and the Sokal "Incident" 109
10. Is a Dialogue Possible? 121
11. Instead of a Conclusion: Fragments for a Book about Interdisciplinarity 133

Preface

This book originates in two "interdisciplinary" experiences I had during the last decade. One was my participation in discussions concerning the curriculum for a new graduate program in the area of cognitive sciences at the Hebrew University in Jerusalem. The question we heatedly debated was how much physics, neurobiology, and computer science a candidate should know for a Ph.D. degree in the interdisciplinarity program to be created. A few years later, I was invited to lecture about science to gifted and talented undergraduates in humanities and social sciences. Being a professor of physics, I assume that the expectation was that I would give some sort of an introduction to elementary modern physics, with the hope that it would be general and simple enough so that the students would understand something about the mechanisms of scientific thinking. Luckily, I had a colleague who agreed to do just this for the length of one semester; as a result, I decided to try to discuss during the second semester the very nature of our interaction: Why would it be of interest for students in humanities and social sciences to understand the way of thinking and the methods of the natural sciences? Would they be able to use any of these methods in their research? Would such an attempt be beneficial, or on the contrary, would it only entangle them in a web of complications, or even worse, would it set them on wrong paths and lead them into blind alleys?

Specialization, or strict confinement within the borders of well-defined disciplines, is a reality of intellectual endeavor in all areas of contemporary academic research. To a large extent this situation is imposed by the methods and the methodology of the research itself, by the immensity of the accumulated knowledge; but there is also some snobbishness and jealousy involved, and in some cases even "caste interests" might have a role to play. On the other hand, it is obvious that there are many areas of research in which the interpenetration at various levels is imposing itself, in an almost natural way. Statistical methods and mathematics for example, are frequently used in social sciences, economics, and medicine. More and more often physics "extends" into chemistry, which in turn merges with biology, in order to create biochemistry. Today, we try to understand many complex phenomena, in both natural and social environments, which can be studied using concepts and methods specific to complex dynamic systems far from equilibrium. Moreover, ideas such as those of "prediction" and "predictability" must be redefined in meteorology, or in the study of the behavior of stock markets, as well as in many other domains.

One can find many examples of successful interdisciplinarity; but for each such example, one may find another one in which the interdisciplinarian effort ended if not in catastrophe, then at best with inconclusive results. By "catastrophe," I mean a falsification of the scope and the results of the research, the creation of an impression of "scientificity." A few examples of both kinds will be discussed in this book. What is worrisome is the fact that "bad interdisciplinarity" may lead to posturing, which in turn transforms entire areas of intellectual endeavor into incomprehensible verbiage. That point too will be touched on in the book. As my discussion with the students progressed, it became clear that the question shifted from *What is it and how does one practice interdisciplinarity?* to *What makes interdisciplinarity possible and/or desirable?* Once this question was posed, my attention shifted to the meaning of "interdisciplinarity" itself. From the trivial observation that the concept of "interdisciplinarity" includes that of "discipline," follows that in order to understand the first, we must understand the second. This trivial observation triggered my reflections upon the nature of the disciplines and their historical development. These in turn, led to the idea of *disciplinarian thinking*. This way of thinking is related to "scientific reasoning," but the two are not identical. Disciplinarian thinking has a more general character, it permeates scientific reasoning, but it applies not only to the "hard" sciences; by its very "nature," it is inducive of "compartimentalization." The first part of this book deals with this matter; in fact, at some point I wanted to entitle the book *A Critique of Disciplinarian Thinking*, but since it was too reminiscent of the works of famous authors, I stayed with the original title. Since *disciplinarian thinking* results from the coupling of certain types of concepts through quantitative operations (mathematics), in order to create genuine "interdisciplinarian thinking," one must change both the nature of the concepts and the ways in which they are connected. This means that a new kind of logic would have to be introduced, one which can handle the paradoxical and the qualitative. However, concepts and logic are necessary but not sufficient conditions for the creation of a worldview. A certain *purpose*, an *intention*, motivated by either religious or rational beliefs, must be imposed upon the pair "concepts-logic;" a *teleology* (even if not always explicitly recognized) must be at work. It is possible that an understanding based on a new set of concepts, logic and teleology, could bring us beyond the present *disciplinarian thinking*.

Through examples of successful or failed "interdisciplinarity," through the presentation of ideas of philosophers and scientists, from Leibnitz to Husserl, concerning the possibility of humanistic, economic, and social sciences, I tried to establish a frame for the discussion concerning *interdisciplinarity*. I must however clearly express here my belief that interdisciplinarity as understood and practiced today is not a miraculous solution to all the difficulties we encounter while trying to understand the complex world we inhabit. Neither is compartmentalization, the division into disciplines, the "monster" we must rid ourselves of, as some postmodernist authors seem to think. This book is meant to represent a first step, an introduction, a contribution toward the creation of a frame for the discussions around the question concerning interdisciplinarity in a world of increasing complexity. In the original plan for the book, I included a few chapters concerning the problem of *complexity*. As I was writing them, I realized that this is another stage in the work I started here, and I decided to defer this problem to a second volume. On the other hand, as this work progressed, I realized the controversial nature of the subject under discussion. I must confess that when I began writing, it was not clear to me to what extent even the concept of "interdisciplinarity" was controversial. But as I already said, interdisciplinarity poorly understood and badly practiced leads to nonsensical intellectual constructs which deepen the disciplinarian divide. The "explosion," announced in the fifties by C.P. Snow in his *Two Cultures*, "hit" us quite violently with the publication in 1996 of Alan Sokal's paper in *Social Text*, followed a year later by the book by Sokal and Bricmont, *Fashionable Nonsense*. I tried to avoid becoming part of the controversy between the representatives of "hard" sciences and humanists involved in postmodernist cultural studies and sociology of science; still, I had to briefly touch on the subject since it is relevant to the discussion of *disciplinarian thinking*.

Along the way I discovered with surprise some unexpected "traveling companions," from early Greek and Chinese philosophers to modern critics of rational thinking such as Lev Shestov or the Zen Buddhist philosopher, Nishida Kitaro. Besides and beyond the famous practitioners of interdisciplinarity, from Aristotle to Bachelard, I discovered others, lesser known, such as Matte Blanco or Stephane Lupasco. An endless number of books have been written about that turning point called the *Galilean-Newtonian revolution*; when I briefly discussed the subject, I preferred to follow its description more or less as presented by a little known—outside the borders of his native

Romania—philosopher, Lucian Blaga, in an attempt to introduce to the English-speaking public this deep and prolific thinker (some of his works have recently been translated into French). And this point brings me to the problem of sources and references: in a book like this, the number of citations and the sources accumulate at an amazing rate. I tried to keep the quotes at a minimum, and in many cases I cited not the most authoritative works on the subject under discussion, but those which I considered most accessible to the student (and to the general reader). Sometimes I found older books more didactic than the most recent texts on the subject. As a general rule, I tried not to encumber the text with too many footnotes, in order to make the argumentation transparent and the reading easier for the—by definition—unspecialized reader. I had to keep in mind at all times that when we talk about interdisciplinarity, nobody is an expert. At the end of the book, I added an appendix, including some scattered thoughts and quotes accumulated while writing. I included these fragments to better illustrate some ideas and authors discussed, or perhaps, to hint at ideas and authors I did not discuss in my book.

Finally, I would like to thank my colleagues at the Hebrew University G. Strumza and I. Unna, who set up the frame for this activity, as well as all my students in these interdisciplinary courses who, during two academic years, helped "filter out" the main ideas expressed in this book. Discussions with friends scattered over the entire world, the late Bill Kluback in New York, Ricardo Nirnberg and Katherine Verdery, François Lurçat and Basarab Nicolescu in France, Piero Boitani in Rome, as well as my friends Yakov Schultz, Leon Volovici, and Monique Jutrin in Israel, are kindly acknowledged. Also, I want to acknowledge the encouragement and help of Japanese colleagues and friends, Takashi Fujimoto, Shoichi Uchii (Kyoto University), Hiroshi Toyama (Tokyo University), Wayne Yokoyama and Mariko Sumikura in Kyoto. My thanks are due also for the great hospitality of my friends and colleagues in the Department of Physics and Astronomy at Johns Hopkins University, in particular Warren Moos and Paul Feldman, and to Heidi Burns, Peter Lang's editor in Baltimore, who initiated the project and waited patiently for its (partial) completion.

Baltimore, January 2000

1

Introduction

In a relatively recent "postmodern proposal," David Ray Griffin, the editor of the series Constructive Postmodern Thought at SUNY, remarks that "the existence of modern society for even another century seems doubtful."[1] Modernism has to be replaced with postmodernism which, we are told, is more of a "diffuse sentiment" than a "common set of doctrines." There is consensus among the different proponents of postmodernism that both *"modernism* in the sense of the worldview that has developed out of the seventeenth-century Galilean-Cartesian-Baconian-Newtonian science, and *modernity* in the sense of the world order that both conditioned and was conditioned by this worldview" belong to the past, and something new and different must replace them. The above are fairly clear definitions; unambiguous is also the postmodernist declaration of intent. I shall examine later in more detail the various definitions and meanings of the terms *modernism, modernity, postmodernism;* at this point I will use the above to state as clearly as possible the purpose of my book. Before doing so however, I will follow a bit further the lead offered by Griffin in his classification of the postmodernist approaches. One such approach, writes Griffin, is the *deconstructive* or *eliminative postmodernism* which "overcomes the modern worldview through an anti-worldview: it deconstructs or eliminates the ingredients necessary for a worldview, such as God, self, purpose, meaning, a real world, and truth as correspondence." The second, is the *constructive* or the *revisionary,* one. It aims at constructing a new view "through a revision of modern premises and traditional concepts."

There is therefore a worldview originating in the "seventeenth-century Galilean-Cartesian-Baconian-Newtonian science"—others have named it the *Galilean-Newtonian (GN) revolution* or simply, the *scientific*

---

[1] David Ray Griffin, ed., *The Reenchantment of Science* (New York: State University of New York Press 1988), p. x.

revolution. Constructive or deconstructive, any "postmodern" attitude requires a thorough understanding of the nature of this "revolution." It is difficult to disagree with those who claim that a new worldview is needed to cope with a more and more complex world. It is hard to see however how we are going to transcend—as the prophets of the postmodernist creed request—the individualism, anthropocentrism, patriarchy, mechanization, economism, consumerism, and militarism of the old worldview, if we continue to remain attached to old ways of thinking. We sense an inner contradiction in the postmodernist arguments: science is based on the postulate that our knowledge of nature is objective. Modernism, the outcome of this objective, reductionist science, has to be replaced by the new postmodernist view, because we have to transcend all the above-mentioned negative byproducts of modernity; but why do we have to transcend all the above? Why do we have to give up the individualism, the anthropocentrism, etc.? In other words, why do we have to replace modernism and modernity? Because of the practical difficulties created by ecological problems? Or because of the extreme forms of mechanized cruelty and large-scale (political) madness we have witnessed in this century? The first can be solved through further advancements in science and technology, and the second category belongs to an existential malaise, rather than to the scientific approach to the world. Science doesn't have to answer questions about the meaning of the "truths" it discovers. One may ask if the existential malaise is not engendered in the process of the scientific research itself. While the scientist regards in awe and admiration the product of his discovery, behind his shoulder the poet and the philosopher may ask what is all that good for? In a recent play which had a large success with the public, one of the characters says: "We were quite happy with Aristotle's cosmos. Personally, I preferred it...Quarks, quasars—big bangs, black holes—who gives a shit?"[2] Of course, this is not always the reaction of the poet and of the philosopher to science; during the sixteenth century, for instance, "scientific poetry" was extensively practiced in France. Pope was an admirer of Newton, and Goethe was as much a poet as a scientist. The nineteenth century strived to make any intellectual endeavor into a science. Humanities and arts were on the way to becoming *Geisteswissenschaften*. Perhaps the failure of the positivist project is at the origin of the doubt concerning a modernity built upon the scientific revolution. But why did the "positivist project" fail? Perhaps the secret lies in *the nature of our patterns of thought* on which the old worldview was built. The worldview based on the *GN revolution* seems to lose its ability

---

[2]Tom Stoppard, *Arcadia* (London: Faber and Faber 1995), p. 61.

to handle the "reality" we live in, but not because science had become too restrictive. It is true, science assumed the reality of an absolute truth; it is true also that the new science requested verification through repeatable experimentation in all possible cases. Moreover, it also tended to restrict itself to the domain of the "physical." But beyond all these there was a certain methodology and well-defined operational concepts which were developed to cope with its objectives. In time, this mixture of specific concepts and specific methodology became a pattern of thought: in the following I shall call this pattern, which has permeated all the domains of Western thought, the disciplinarian way of thinking or, *disciplinarian thinking*. Philosophy, in particular that of Descartes and Leibnitz, was the "crystallizing element" (like the "developer" in the production of photographic prints) in the process, but philosophy played also, later on, the role of the "fixer" (to use the same photographic metaphor) through the French Enlightenment, Kant and German classical philosophy. Today we discover that *disciplinarian thinking* seems to be unable to cope with the complexity which is overwhelming us. The science built upon it, itself produced complexity at an exponentially increasing pace; like spiders, we spun the threads of a magnificent web, only to find ourselves completely entangled in it. For while we have developed a way of thinking which enabled us to create the web, we may have lost sight of that knowledge which could keep us out of it (if we ever had it; some would say that this is precisely the task for the future).

Disciplinarian thinking facing a world of increasing complexity; this is the main theme of this book. The postulate of the increasing complexity is assumed in this work, since the effort is directed rather toward the analysis of the successes and failures of *disciplinarian thinking* as illustrated by the discussion of different interdisciplinarian efforts. In the following chapters I will consider the question of whether the intellectual tools in our possession are adequate for the new odyssey through the labyrinth of complexity we perhaps unwillingly embarked on. There is no need to divide the world into "modern" and "postmodern"; for there is continuity both in this process of growth of complexity and in the continuous development of disciplinarian thinking. As with modernism-modernity-postmodernity, we need to define in as rigorous a way as possible, the key concepts used above, "complexity," "chaos," "disciplinarian thinking"; at this point however I would like to suggest that we all have the intuitive feeling that "complexity" permeates both our personal and professional lives. From the choices we have to make between the drug we take to ease a bad headache, to the difficulty in making the last electronic "gimmick" we have purchased work, we are torn between (too) many choices and exhausted by (too) complicated mental activities. The world seems to be driven by forces which are "chaotic," by mysterious forces upon which our lives seem to be totally dependent: unexplained weather patterns, the stock-market fluctuations in a remote country, or the disappearance, due to some unknown, unexpected, and most of the time incomprehensible technological breakthroughs, of the trade in which we were involved for years, leave us often baffled and sometimes, why deny it, quite scared.

In response, we tend to blame our ways of thinking, to claim that they have become inadequate and/or unable to cope with the new situations, both at the practical as well as at the intellectual, abstract level. As our "scientific thinking" produces more and more complexity (by solving old problems at the price of creating new ones), our traditional ways to cope with it are failing. Is *disciplinarian thinking* to be blamed for our inability to cope with a complex and chaotic world? Is any form of *inter-, intra- or transdisciplinarity* going to "save us," to show us the way to the paradise lost? These seem to me to be the questions any modern Diogenes, riding on the crest of the wave of modernity, should ask.

I am aware that by attempting to discuss *the nature* of disciplinarian thinking, I may be accused of committing a grave error when judged in an "eliminative" or "deconstructionist" postmodernist frame of reference. There are no longer such things as "nature," "essence," or "intrinsic quality" of an object or an idea. We should be very careful about the use of "old" philosophical constructs, we are told; for instance, Max Weber wrote extensively about the social and political implications of scientific research in ancient as well as in modern times. Griffin, the author I quoted above, pointed out in the same work that at the root of modernity and its discontents lies what Max Weber called "the disenchantment of the world." What are we supposed to do with such a concept as that of the "Hellenic man," whose thinking was "political throughout," according to Weber? There were certainly men in ancient Greece for whom a question such as How should a citizen act? was the most important question of their lives. When Weber claims that "for these reasons (political consciousness, the need to practice 'virtue,' etc.) one engaged in science," I feel compelled to try to understand what he means, even if "absolutes" and "grand narratives" are considered dead and buried. Besides, my training in "hard" sciences has taught me that I must define from the very beginning the target of my investigation, "disciplinarian thinking," even if I have to commit heresy. The "confrontation" with the basic tenets of postmodernism will have to come later.

A *discipline* is more than a field of intellectual endeavor defined by the object of its research. It implies also the ability to transfer knowledge in an "objective" way, that is, in such a way that anybody in possession of certain tools can understand it, anywhere and at any time. That is because within a discipline meaning is conserved. In addition, the definition of a discipline requires a logic which enables a consistent handling of its concepts. If this logic is applicable to another set of concepts, an interdisciplinarian relation can be established between the two domains. According to such an argument, mathematics was a "discipline" since ancient times. When applied—by the Pythagoreans—to cosmology or music, it led to the earliest "interdisciplinarian" endeavors. But this observation may introduce some confusion into our discussion since it raises the question Is mathematics a "discipline" or rather an "interdisciplinarian tool"? As we shall see, both Descartes and Leibnitz addressed this question in detail. It thus becomes evident that even at this early stage of the discussion a definition is needed, and at the same time it is clear that an accurate definition of the concept of "discipline" is not easy. As a result, it will be even more difficult to define "interdisciplinarity" in a rigorous way. That is why in my exposition, I have chosen to adopt the "jumbo-jet takeoff approach": we shall move gently and slowly toward the focal point of our discussion. Instead of rushing for definitions, we shall follow the unfolding of the story of the birth of *disciplinarian thinking* in the Western world. This is the story of a gradual emergence through a very long process which began with the pre-Socratics and ended with what we call the *GN revolution*. At times we will shift somewhat the spotlights and focus on the period between the end of the Middle Ages and that preceding the scientific revolution. Under this spotlight we shall watch the activities of a few lesser known actors, some of them scholastic philosophers, some alchemists and magicians in addition to being philosophers and theologians. All played a very important role in the establishment of the *disciplinarian thinking* which made the GN revolution possible. This new way of thinking, which we should remember is ours too, is based on a very peculiar methodology and a select class of concepts capable of operating within the confines of a *mathesis universalis*. *Disciplinarian thinking* requires therefore a special methodology, but also specific types of concepts adequate to this methodology. In putting forward this idea I am to a large extent, as mentioned in the preface, in debt to a great Romanian philosopher, very little known to the West, Lucian Blaga. In various places in my work I shall try to present some of his ideas relevant to our discussion; it is a pity that—to the best of my knowledge—none of his works have been translated into English; all the quotations offered in the present work are my translation from the original Romanian texts. Blaga claimed that in addition to the emergence of experimental research, the GN revolution was to a large extent due to a change in the concepts used to interpret the experimental data: only those concepts which were quantifiable and amenable to mathematical handling were retained in Galilean and Newtonian physics. Moreover, a "supermethod," as Blaga called it, was instated for the benefit of all those involved in natural philosophy, which consisted of "censoring" and rejecting any nonquantifiable concept from scientific research. Blaga doesn't tell us who invented this "supermethod" or how it imposed itself upon the minds of the protagonists of the GN revolution. I will argue here that what made the GN revolution possible was much more than the emergence of a few new operational concepts and a new methodology; the slowly emerging *disciplinarian thinking*, of course, included these but it was much more: it was the dream of the *mathesis universalis* come true. Among other things, it assimilated and included in itself that "tendency toward unification, characteristic of the modern man" Ernst Cassirer was talking about. It made also possible the separation between the immanent, the new object of inquiry, and the transcendent. *Disciplinarian thinking* is not contemplative, it doesn't want only to ascertain the known or the intuited, it is also a thinking in permanent search for novelty. Its methodology is not only that of quantitative research but also that of a research which enables new and unexpected discoveries. Was Galileo Galilei already a "disciplinarian" thinker according to these definitions? Probably not. One may have doubts about Newton too in that respect. But the process which started during the seventeenth century consolidated during the eighteenth; by the nineteenth century, positivistic science and philosophy were already totally "disciplinarian." Exceptions were, of course, a few Romantic thinkers (from Blake to Kierkegaard and Nietzsche). The twentieth century marked the beginning of serious and more and more systematic revolt against disciplinarian thinking, perceived as the "tyranny of reason."

This book contains both a critique of disciplinarian thinking and its brief history as well. While the "critique" is scattered over the entire book, the "history" is concentrated in the next three chapters. Chapter 2 discusses the origins, and since in the beginning was the concept, we start with Socrates and Plato. The concept as developed by these two philosophers enables us to single out ideas, categories, "essences," universals on which we can operate through logical thinking, or examine through experimentation, and thus arrive at "truths." It should be noted that from the very beginning, the One was needed to gain some control over the Many; multiplicity is difficult to grasp, is "chaotic." A *circle* is the essential form of many "round" objects; *heaviness* seems to be an intrinsic property of any material body. But then such is *lightness* also. Aristotle concluded that there are heavy bodies and light ones. The next step was to say something meaningful about the concepts: to find predicates for these subjects, which will further our knowledge, such as "heavy bodies fall, light ones levitate." What would have enabled the thinker to add "always"? To begin with, experience or experimentation. But the clever philosopher quickly discovered that experience tells us only that "so far we observe that heavy bodies always fall"; can we infer from that they will *always* do the same? Not necessarily, according to Aristotle. We must invoke some fundamental principles (postulates), such as that of the final cause (entelechy), in order to overcome such uncertainties. These principles represent absolute truths, independent of the thinking mind. (At this point I must remind the reader that this is not a book on the history of philosophy; at times I will make statements which will be correct in a given context, but which will not always be followed up to the farthest points reached at later times in different contexts. Thus, for instance, the last sentence has been deeply modified by Heidegger; moreover, he claimed that the origin of his philosophy is to be find in the pre-Socratics, etc.) We find thus in Aristotle a philosophy built upon concepts linked together by a self-consistent logic. The Stagirite is very important to our discussion for at least two reasons: one, he is the founder of ancient Greek science and two, when rediscovered in the early Middle Ages, the scholastic and postscholastic interpretations of his philosophy, influenced profoundly the ways of thinking which were to lead to the "new science," that born of the NG revolution. It is strange however that between the Greek science and that of the moderns, a gap of about two thousand years exists. What was missing in this impressive body of knowledge, so that Western civilization had to wait so long for its next scientific revolution to occur? Why did the very technically minded Roman civilization, for instance, not take advantage of Aristotelian physics and bring it to the point reached (so many) centuries later by Galileo and Newton?

Something essential was missing, and deep changes in the ways of thinking had to evolve before modern science could be born. It was not merely a "liberation" from the scholastic-Aristotelian tradition, as some seem to believe. The road to these changes, which occurred in the fifteenth and sixteenth centuries, was paved by the gradual changes brought to the Greek ways of thinking by the emerging, and later the developing, Christian theology (through the "true philosophers," as they were called in their own tradition) from Clement of Alexandria, Tertullian, and Origen to St. Thomas. This process continued through medieval scholasticism which ended in the quarrel between the "nominalists" and the "realists," further developed in the interaction between the magical or "alchemistic thinking" of the late Middle Ages, and finally, it was brought close to completion by the humanists of the fourteenth and fifteenth centuries, from Petrarca to Montaigne. Of course, the medieval Muslim and Jewish thinkers made their contribution too. As a scholar writing about the Italian Renaissance pointed out, "The Aristotelian tradition of natural philosophy was not overthrown by the outside attacks of the humanists or Platonists, nor by suggestive theories of the natural philosophers. It yielded only in and after the seventeenth century, when the new science of Galileo and his successors was able to deal with its subject matter on the basis of a firmly established and superior method."[3] The issues concerning the "suggestive theories of the natural philosophers" and, perhaps more importantly, that of the "firmly established, superior method" will be discussed in the second and third chapters of the book.

In order to emphasize through contrast some of the characteristic milestones of the evolution toward "disciplinarian thinking" in the West, the fourth chapter is dedicated to the Far East, a very brief and superficial overview of the question Why did the Far East not have its scientific revolution? This has often been asked, and various answers have been attempted. I tried to answer the question keeping in mind the concept of disciplinarian thinking as central to determining the direction of the argumentation. The first part of the book ends with the conclusion that a *disciplinarian thinking* has emerged in Western civilization, and after the GN revolution, it took over every aspect of its intellectual activities. To this very day, we still think and act within its confines. The rigidity of its methodology has created invisible walls around all domains of research. At first, the "reality" was such that one could afford them; moreover, in the beginning one needed these walls in order to develop science to its highest level of performance and to create its ultimate corollary, modern technology. However, "reality" itself changed in the process: while the newly developed science could cope more and more efficiently with the natural world open to its inspection, the progress of technology brought an increased complexity in an ever expanding man-created reality. In addition, the uncovering of many "mysteries" of the natural world added tremendously to the sum total of our knowledge, thus increasing the overall complexity of this combined, *natural and man-created world*, linked today by a new, "virtual reality."

Interdisciplinarity, in the sense I wish to use this concept, represents the attempt to overcome the barriers imposed by disciplinarian thinking. We do not have to sacrifice the sacred cow of modernity because it created inequalities through its "absolutes." We do not have to relativize everything just because it sounds more democratic to say that nothing has intrinsic absolute value and every construct of the mind or any social

---

[3]Paul O. Kristeller, *Eight Philosophers of the Italian Renaissance* (Stanford: Stanford University Press, 1964), p. 96.

order have equal value and an equal right to exist under the sun. Disciplinarian thinking is not bad because it perpetuates some obsolete ways of thinking which must be replaced with newer and more progressive ones. Interdisciplinarity must not become a "revolutionary tool" in a war of ideologies. Interdisciplinarity is needed for two reasons: one is to enable us to cope with complexity and the other is to prevent excessive divisions within our cultures. A simplistic version of it, rooted in disciplinarian thinking, will not fulfill any of these tasks. We must therefore analyze the concept in an honest and uncompromising way, in order to find out what interdisciplinarity is and what it is not. That is the purpose of the second part of the book.

Disciplinarian thinking is reductionist. Complexity cannot be studied with tools developed essentially for a reductionist approach. Today there are certain research areas in physics (and other fields such as computer science, artificial intelligence, cognitive science) which try to study complexity using intellectual devices developed for specific problems related to nonlinear, far-from-equilibrium systems. The point is that even the best tools fail us if used in a **context** which is not appropriate. And the context of most present-day research has been defined by the GN revolution: it is the context of disciplinarian thinking. It won't help to merely use laws of physics in cognitive sciences or economy, or to try to quantify concepts belonging to the social or humanistic fields of research through the use of statistics or some sort of simple algebra. This is just poor mimicking of the scientific approach. What is needed is a new way of thinking which shatters the walls of disciplinarian thinking.

The fact is that there is a "practical" interdisciplinarity at work in almost any area of intellectual endeavor. Even in a "hard science" such as physics, one can find the traces of metaphors or ideas coming from elsewhere: grand unification theory, action at distance, etc. With some surprise we will encounter in a physics journal a paper concerning the use of "neural network" techniques in fast pattern or spectra recognition; what exactly does this mean? "Neural networks" seem to belong to biology, we remember having been taught that they enable us to interact with the surrounding world; they are the fabric of "sensorial perception." But how can they be used in other contexts? By whom? Where? In what form? No less surprised are we to find that behind the neoclassical theory of the economists lies the Hamilton-Jacobi formalism developed by physicists in theoretical mechanics. Schrödinger, one of the greatest physicist of the century (one of the founding fathers of quantum mechanics), wrote a book entitled *What is Life?*[4] which fifty years later

---

[4]Erwin Schrödinger, *What Is Life?* (Cambridge: Cambridge University Press, 1967).

biologists revisited with great respect.[5] The examples of interdisciplinarian interactions seem endless. Still, the extension of a method from one discipline to another or the use of common metaphors represents a "weak" interdisciplinarity, or something one could call "mechanical interdisciplinarity." There is no real common denominator, no genuine fusion between activities far apart from an intellectual point of view. Disciplinarian thinking imposes its rigid divisions and patterns of thought upon this kind of interdisciplinarity. This fact is reflected in the permanent tension between the "two cultures," which at times, becomes—as we have already observed—explosive. Under the appearances of unification through interdisciplinarity, the deep divides are maintained.

Carl Hempel described the situation well: human sciences, he wrote, could be made "scientific" *if* they managed *somehow* to incorporate the explanatory methods of natural sciences. *Somehow*. In many cases some sort of a formalization of the discourse, the introduction of mathematical formulas, seemed to be the simplest ways to mimic the scientific approach. Scientists and philosophers of science have often attacked these procedures, considered by them, at the best, naive forms of interdisciplinarity. Thus, in a recent collection of papers entitled *The Flight from Science and Reason*,[6] Mario Bunge sharply attacks the "academic pseudoscience" and gives examples of *pseudomathematical symbolism* and *pseudoquantification* found in the works of such important figures in classical sociology as Pareto and Sorokin. In recent times, the phenomenon is identified in the works of the political scientist Samuel Huntington or the economists Gary Backer and Milton Freedman. An alert and well-versed reader will observe however that there is nothing new under the sun: Hugo Grotius, a great admirer of Galileo's mathematical accomplishments in (what was then called) natural philosophy, wrote his *De jure belli et pacis* (published in 1625) in the manner of a book of geometry (much before Spinoza, who was born in 1632!). Or another example from old times: James Harrington's politico-social oeuvre (which later was to influence the American founding fathers) was presented in *Oceana* (1656)—under the influence of Harvey's studies on animal generation—as a *political anatomy*. And what to say about young Leibnitz, who published a mathematical demonstration of the method for selecting the best candidate to become the...king of Poland!

---

[5]M.P. Murphy and L.A.J. O'Neill, eds., *What Is Life? The Next Fifty Years* (New York: Cambridge University Press, 1995).
[6]P.R. Gross, N. Levitt, and M.W. Lewis, eds., *The Flight from Science and Reason* (Baltimore: Johns Hopkins University Press, 1996).

The interdisciplinarity practiced in "hard" sciences meant in most cases the transfer of a certain concept, technique, or mathematical construct from one domain of research to another. For instance, in trying to understand the processes through which energy is transformed in living organisms, physics, chemistry, biophysics, and biochemistry are used simultaneously. Physicists, computer scientists, and neurophysiologists work together in trying to explain neuronal transmission and image recognition by the human brain. The success of this type of interdisciplinarian approach is tested through experiments and their results. If as a result of an interdisciplinary approach I can modify a process or build an artificial device which will work as well as a "natural" one, I will declare the effort successful or the results of the investigation correct. The interdisciplinary approach was successful. What if I use a concept taken from one domain not as an "operational" concept, but simply as a metaphor, hoping to clarify certain ideas in a quite different domain? Is this interdisciplinarity, too? For instance, economists used the concept of "equilibrium," and a related physical theory, to create economic models aimed at explaining quantitatively processes related to market dynamics. In all cases of "weak interdisciplinarity," which—I must remind the reader—is the case in *any* interdisciplinarian effort made within the framework of disciplinarian thinking, the proof must be in the pudding. But in cases in which the experimental tests are difficult or even impossible, it is hard to judge the effectiveness of the interdisciplinarian approach, not to mention its "truthfulness." There are extreme examples (such as those quoted by Bunge in the book mentioned above), to which I shall return later; let me illustrate my point here with an example based on this quote from Jean Baudrillard: "Dans l'espace euclidien de l'histoire, le chemin le plus rapide d'un point à un autre est la ligne droite, celle du Progrès et de la Démocratie."[7] There is therefore a "space" occupied by history—which is essentially temporal—and this "space" is Euclidean. To those of us who have heard of the "curvature of the non-Euclidean space-time" in Einstein's theory of (general) relativity, the image is very suggestive. There is a classical time in history dominated by simple, linear relationships, where the "norm" is that of progress and democracy. We expect to hear, that a "relativistic sociopolitical history" will determine a new "space of history," a nonlinear one, having different "metrics," granted, difficult to define but certainly not the old one, that of progress and democracy. Indeed, Baudrillard continues and defines our times as "the non-Euclidean space of the end of the century," dominated by an evil curvature (courbure maléfique). This curvature bends, diverts, and

---

[7]Jean Baudrillard, *L'Illusion de la fin* (Paris: Galilée, 1992), p. 23.

corrupts all the possible trajectories, according to Baudrillard. What can be said about the "truth content" of such statements? What is new in them, beyond the metaphor?

Interdisciplinarity can become very detrimental when practiced loosely. Forty years ago, C.P. Snow expressed in *The Two Cultures and the Scientific Revolution* [8] his concern that the two dominant cultures of the Western tradition, one stemming from the scientific worldview, the other from the humanistic approach, are on a head-on collision track. It was the mutual incomprehension the author—a scientist by training, a writer by vocation—feared. Snow recognized implicitly that both cultures essentially shared the same type of thinking (in our parlance, *disciplinarian thinking*). It was not that people thought differently, they talked different languages. It was the "Babel syndrome" at work. The key words were *incomprehension* and *different attitudes*. No different ways of thinking were involved really. In chapter 7 of the book, I write that the conflict described by Snow had its origin in the situation created toward the end of the centuries-long fight between the nominalists and the realists of scholastic philosophy. As the dispute died away, in spite of the appearances, there was only one issue left for debate: that of the knowledge of *reality*. Whether this was the reality of the ideal forms, of the content of our concepts, or that of the concrete, the immanent, has become, de facto, less important. The main (and only) purpose of human intellectual endeavor had become *the search for the "real,"* regardless its definition. The concepts and the methodologies used had to be optimized for success in that direction. That is the origin of the *disciplinarian thinking*. In the circumstances of its birth we find also the reason why, in spite of all the divisions and the animosities expressed at the level of the discourse, *disciplinarian thinking* has evolved into the common modality of thinking of both scientists and humanists in their pursuit of "reality." This situation perpetuates itself to this very day. The "Sokal story"[9] (see chapter 9) and the reactions on both sides reflect the same "Babel syndrome": they are the result of a failed interdisciplinarity; for I will claim that within the confines of *disciplinarian thinking*, any interdisciplinarian effort which tries to go beyond the ideals of *mathesis universalis* is bound to fail. *Within the realm of disciplinarian thinking only a limited and well-defined kind of interdisciplinarity is possible* ("*weak interdisciplinarity*"). The second part of the book addresses these problems. I hope that this way of stating the problem of interdisciplinarity not only avoids the quarrel between postmodernism

---

[8]C.P. Snow, *The Two Cultures and the Scientific Revolution* (New York: Cambridge University Press).
[9]Alan Sokal and Jean Bricmont, *Impostures intellectuelles* (Paris: Odile Jacob, 1997).

and modernity but also overcomes, the more technical debate between the poststructuralists, who claim that disciplinarian (or departmental) divisions do not make sense in the context of "complex human systems," and certain academic quarters which reject any form of interdisciplinarity, considering them a dilettante effort at best. In the context of the ideas expressed here, this quarrels are simply irrelevant.

2

The Greek Way to Disciplinarian Thinking

Windelband called Parmenides the "scientific founder of the Eleatic school."[1] Why would he consider this proponent of the abstract concept of Being, the founder of ontology and metaphysics, "scientific"? In what sense was Parmenides "scientific"? Perhaps Windelband saw in him a precursor of Aristotle because of his ontological rejection of the void; or he found him "scientific" because of the rudiments of a physical theory he identified in the second part of the only two fragments by the philosopher in our possession (*The Way of Truth* and *The Way of Seeming*). Perhaps Windelband believed that the abstract (conceptual) reasoning announced by Parmenides, "the forerunner of Platonic idealism," was the only way to achieve scientific truth. An interesting answer to some of these questions has been given by Carl Friederich von Weizsäcker—a contemporary, "politically active professor of philosophy trained as a physicist," as he defined himself—in a long essay entitled "Parmenides and Quantum Theory."[2] Weizsäcker considered both the fragments mentioned and Plato's dialogue *Parmenides* in his attempt to understand the Eleatic philosopher's thought. After a detailed discussion of the concept of "unity" and the nature of "the One" in quantum mechanics, he reached the conclusion that the "One" of the physicists is identical to that of Parmenides. Windelband, who lived in a world dominated by "scientism" and a positivism striving to make any intellectual endeavor into a science, could not have been so specific; at the time, natural sciences were still dominated by the ideas of classical physics. He

---

[1] Wilhelm Windelband, *History of Ancient Philosophy* (New York: Dover Publications, 1956), p. 59.
[2] Carl Friederich von Weizsäcker, *The Unity of Nature* (New York: Farrar, Straus and Giroux, 1980).

contented himself with claiming that Greek science began with Parmenides, achieved maturity during the fourth century B.C., and reached its zenith in Aristotle. What followed during the Hellenic-Roman period was just an "after-effect." He considered the latter to be a period in which the "product of philosophical principles and fundamental concepts is very small" and during which "scientific activity was turned to special researches, and found neutral ground partly in nature studies, partly in history."[3] I shall not discuss here the idea of the "neutral ground" interesting in itself, but will rather hasten to follow Windelband's argumentation: "This ardent cultivation of the special sciences had the most universal results of Greek philosophy for its obviously valid fundamental principles."[4] That is, what followed insofar as scientific developments in the Hellenistic-Roman world were concerned was entirely based on the epistemological and the ontological ideas and principles worked out by classical Greek philosophy. The conclusion is that "erudition pressed out the spirit of speculation. The special sciences became independent."[5] That would be, therefore, the origin of the scientific disciplines. For Windelband, the *disciplinarian thinking* is a consequence of the "fall" of the Greek philosophy; at the same time, it is recognized as being rooted in the conceptual ground created by classical Greece.

Before continuing the discussion about the origins of the *disciplinarian thinking*, I must observe that any such discussion is held on somewhat shaky grounds: it has often been pointed out that our understanding of ideas and concepts originating in a culture very different from ours is problematic. The "dangers" involved in the interpretation of a thinking belonging to a different age, developed in a very different cultural context, were present in the minds of the scholars long before the postmodernist times dominated by relativism and deconstructionist trends. F.M. Cornford ("a historian and a poet" as W.K.C. Guthrie, another distinguished Greek scholar, respectfully called him) often warned about the "dangers besetting the task of recovering what the ancient philosophers meant" and pointed out that when and if we attempt this task, we must recall that the "ancients were not moderns in the stage of infancy or adolescence."[6] The temptation is great and mistakes have been made by many. Thus for instance, Werner Heisenberg, another of the founding fathers of modern physics, wrote,

---

[3]Windelband, p. 295.
[4]Ibid.
[5]Ibid.
[6]Francis M. Cornford, *The Unwritten Philosophy and Other Essays* (Cambridge: Cambridge University Press, 1967), pp. 29, 82.

"We may remark at this point that modern physics is in some way extremely near to the doctrines of Heraclitus."[7] Cautiously or not, coming from philosophers, scientists, or historians, we often end up with the statement that "scientific thought" originates with the pre-Socratics. I find this statement as meaningful as the one claiming that the apple has its origin in the roots of the apple tree; that is, while being a perfectly true statement, it is at the same time a perfectly useless one when we want to characterize an apple and compare it with an orange. Questions about *nature* and *the nature of nature* were posed by Greek philosophers from the pre-Socratics till deep into the Christian era; or as the above mentioned Cornford wrote: "Greek philosophy began when Thales of Miletus predicted an eclipse of the sun in 585 B.C. and ended in A.D. 529 when the Christian Emperor Justinian closed the schools of Athens."[8] But how much "science" was in this philosophy? And was there a "scientific thinking," as we understand it today, within the Greek philosophy? On the other hand, if the Greek "science" was different from ours, how did our science emerge from it? Is there a continuity between us and the ancient Greeks?

In one of the few books on interdisciplinarity I was able to find, the author, Stephen J. Kline, writes in the introductory chapter: "The scientific approach to knowledge since the time of Galileo has provided the human race with a far better understanding of our world and of ourselves than was available to any previous society. This gain in understanding has arisen primarily from two sources. We have adopted what we loosely call, 'the scientific methods' and we have broken the intellectual enterprise into a larger and larger number of parts (disciplines and research programs)."[9] We should therefore talk of *a scientific approach to knowledge*—at least in the context of Western civilization—only from the onset of, and after, the Renaissance. This is an idea widely accepted. Also, the thought that this revolutionary change was brought about by the simultaneous apparition of a "scientific method" and a "breaking of the intellectual enterprise" into disciplines is considered common knowledge. But as we have already seen, the nature and the genesis of this "scientific method" are often misunderstood—and the problem of the disciplines is treated most of the time "mechanically," more or less the way Windelband did it. It is assumed that natural philosophy became *scientific* when mathematics were added to the

---

[7]Werner Heisenberg, *Physics and Philosophy* (London: George Allen and Unwin, 1959), p. 61.
[8]Cornford, p. 81.
[9]Stephen J. Kline, *Conceptual Foundations for Multidisciplinary Thinking* (Stanford: Stanford University Press, 1995).

logical argumentation and more place was accorded to experimentation. One of the main arguments of my work is that although an incipient form of *disciplinarian thinking* existed already in an amorphous state before the Renaissance, its true development began at the onset of what we already called *the GN revolution*. Therefore, what we term "scientific thinking" is essentially the fully developed "disciplinarian thinking" born in modern times. The "disciplines" into which this *disciplinarian thinking* has organized itself are different from the mere compartmentalization of the human intellectual endeavors following the birth of Greek philosophy. By its nature, the scientific knowledge as developed in Western (or Judeo-Christian) civilization, is disciplinarian; as we shall see, our attempts toward inter- or transdisciplinarity are affected and ultimately limited by this fact. A "restoring force" like that caused by the elasticity of a spring will always force us back into the all-encompassing realm of this disciplinarian thinking of ours. As we shall see, there is indeed a somewhat "broken continuity" from the pre-Socratics to our days, throughout the GN revolution, which connects Parmenides (and other ancient Greeks) with modern science. However, such connections are superficial and lack any deeper meaning; at best, they can serve as metaphors of continuity.

We must not confuse the idea of a "specific domain of (intellectual) activity," with the concept of "discipline," as understood in the modern sense. The specificity of an abstract intellectual endeavor stems from an idea of "individuation" expressed clearly for the first by Plato in his *Republic*: "...all things are produced more plentifully and easily and of a better quality, when one *man does one thing which is natural* to him...."[10] In ancient Athens, the answer to the question What should a man (citizen) do? was determined by the postulate that all men have specific abilities, natural tendencies toward well-defined jobs. Max Weber followed this Platonic postulate when he remarked that for the ancient Greeks, the duty toward the city (state) was an imperative: "For the Hellenic man thinking was political throughout." This imposed striving toward the accomplishment of a specific task (which the citizen was destined or suited for) requires in turn an ability to focus on the object of his mission, whether it is physical or spiritual. Was indeed Plato the first one to express this idea? Maybe not; maybe his ancestors adopted it long before him, in the Homeric times when they discovered the notion of *arete*. It is a word we commonly translate as "virtue," but which for the Greeks had a quite different meaning from ours (or the Roman, or the early Jewish-Christian "virtue," perceived as an "active reason" meant to guard and guide us toward the right paths; these later meanings originated

---

[10]*Republic*, 243.

probably in Stoic philosophy). Indeed, it has been pointed out that *arete* meant for the pre-Socratics (and probably until the third century B.C.) *the ability to perform in a proper way a particular task*. Thus, a "virtuous person" was somebody who strived to have a clear understanding of his task, as a prerequisite for its proper fulfillment. That is what Socrates (and Plato) meant when he said (or wrote) "virtue is knowledge"; did Francis Bacon mean the same thing when he himself wrote—almost two thousand years later—"tantum possumus quantum scimus" (our might goes as far as our knowledge)?

Therefore, even if the idea of "specialization" can be traced down to the pre-Socratics, it was clearly formulated for the first time by Plato. This is not too surprising if we remember that—to quote Max Weber again (in his lecture on *Science and Vocation*)—it is between him (Plato) and Socrates that "the *concept*, one of the great tools of all scientific knowledge, has been consciously discovered." If we are to properly perform our tasks, we must clearly single out the object of our study or activity; to do so, we must be able to isolate it, to define it. For Socrates, a crusader in the battle against the Sophists, the concept was just a "logical object," a mental artifact which enabled him to pin down a corresponding fact or event belonging to concrete reality. It was Plato who later on identified the concept with its "reality content." But he went one step further when he proclaimed the concept as the only reality: only what was fixed, constant, and eternal was real. Any manifestation of the surrounding world as perceived through our senses was just an imperfect approximation of the absolute, the transcendent "idea." Aristotle, who was very different from Plato in many ways, has adopted however some of the metaphysical bents of his master, but we must not be confused by his *Metaphysics*. Somebody had remarked that "*Metaphysics* was...no more than a brief interlude in the history of Greek thought. It began with Plato, and it ended with Plato."[11] We shall discuss Aristotle's ideas relevant to our argumentation later; for the moment I wish to continue this brief overview of the progress of "specialized knowledge" in the Greek philosophical realm.

Aristotle's successor at the head of the Lyceum, Theophrastus, seems to have been not only an accomplished "disciplinarian," but also very much inclined toward grounding the natural sciences in observation and experiment, in ways much more rigorous than those proposed by Aristotle. He was skeptical (to put it mildly) about his teacher's teleological views: "With regard to the view that all things are for the sake of an end and nothing is in vain, the assignment of ends is in

---

[11]The quote is from Brian Farrington, *Greek Science* (London: Penguin Books, 1953), p. 155.

general not easy, as it is usually stated to be."[12] Strato, who followed Theophrastus at the head of the Lyceum, and later went to Alexandria to continue at the Museum the tradition of Athens, was already known as "the physicist." In his *Lives and Teachings of the Philosophers*, Diogenes Laertius mentions the forty writings of Strato the physicist; he "excelled in every branch of learning, but most of all in...the philosophy of nature, a branch of philosophy more ancient and serious than the others."[13] But Diogenes Laertius lived at the beginning of the third century A.C. and he was accused of things worse than being biased toward "his" philosophers. Cicero was less enthusiastic about Strato, since he "abandoned ethics, which is the most necessary part of philosophy, and devoted himself to the investigation of nature."[14] We are not interested here in the ethical biases of the two later thinkers, we will observe only that, as Windelband pointed out, a tendency toward disciplinarian divisions seemed to be present everywhere in the Greek, as well as Roman, philosophical realm. Polybius, the Greek historian who lived through the second century B.C. (for many years in Rome), wrote in his *History*, that "all branches of science have now made such progress that instruction in most of them has been systematized."[15] At this stage therefore, *the division into "disciplines" came from the need to systematize an exceeding volume of "specialized thinking," and was not the result of the application of any specific methodology to various domains of intellectual activity.*

Disciplinarian thinking requires in addition to the need for classification (a need which appeared early in human thought—one may want to call this essentially taxonomic thinking "Edenic thinking," in order to distinguish it from the Platonic theory of classification) *a need for purpose* to be attached to the reflexive activity. We think in order to gain knowledge, to understand and through understanding become like God (or gods, in the Greek or Roman context): powerful and in control. In the Bible, the serpent told Adam that already; in the context of Judeo-Christian culture, we might call such thinking, "Exilic" or "post-Edenic" thinking. This *post-Edenic thinking*, while it already has a specialized character, is still far from being yet a *disciplinarian thinking*. It is a thinking which has acquired a sense of purpose and orientation among the various questions raised at the previous taxonomic or Edenic level. It clearly distinguishes between questions related to morality and law, logic and mathematics. It is the path followed by the ancient Greeks

---

[12] Ibid., p. 162.
[13] Quoted in Farrington, p. 172.
[14] Ibid., 171.
[15] Ibid., p. 157.

toward the idea of *truth*, toward the *alétheia*. Once this idea was born, the question of its "nature" followed: How should we know what is true, which is the truth? There is *doxa* and there is *episteme*. At this point, the truth becomes associated with its domain of application, the "discipline" under study. This represented doubtlessly an important step toward *disciplinarian thinking*.

The moment at which we have arrived represents a crossroad in the ancient Greek thinking and deeply influenced its (and other) future philosophical options: Parmenides, by stating that we cannot know but that which exists, that which *is* (*to on*), opened the way toward the "tyranny of truth," as Lev Shestov called it.[16] That which exists is true and true is that which exists—said Parmenides—and thus knowledge (thought) and existence (being) became one. Aristotle, says Shestov, claimed in the *Metaphysics* that Parmenides was "constrained to follow the phenomena" and that he and the rest of the Greek philosophers "were constrained by the truth itself."[17] With the birth of the *constraining truth*, of the *absolute necessity*, the way to scientific inquiry was open. But how was the gap between Parmenides and Aristotle bridged?

The gap was bridged by Socrates. Socrates was nineteen years old when Parmenides was already sixty-five; at the time (c. 450 B.C.), he was still interested in sciences (according to Plato in *Phaedo*), still associated with Archelaos the physicist. However, like Pascal two thousand years later, he abandoned the search for the "truth of the being, of the existing" and replaced it with the inquiry into "the right conduct in life and death." There was no God in Athens (only a poor *daimon*) to guide him on this journey; why then, did he change his route? One cannot help thinking that every age has its "existential" philosophers. "How can we know the reality of being?" Socrates asked. We need concepts; the concept is the logical analogue, the equivalent in thought of the "substance," of the existing object. Therefore Socrates invented the concept. For him the problem was how to establish the elements of permanence in our thinking, the building blocks of consciousness. Not that he was less interested in the rules which governed the process of thought; but those were too close to the Sophists. The concept was the logical simile of the substantial, the material, which exists outside our consciousness. From a logical point of view, Socrates emphasized, without explicitly naming it, the principle of identity; of course, working with concepts required a logic. Some sort of nonformalized logic existed already; it was mainly the logic underlying the activity of the hated

---

[16]Lev Shestov, "Parmenides in Chains" in *Athens and Jerusalem* (New York: Simon and Schuster, 1966).
[17]*Athens and Jerusalem*, p. 77.

Sophists. Their logic was biased toward the ability to demonstrate everything. However, even if the Sophists relativized the truth to a degree which lead to (a sort of) nihilism or extreme skepticism, they brought a very important contribution to the analysis of our ways of thinking. It should be kept in mind that the Sophists were not philosophers, they did not represent a school of thought (even though some, such as Protagoras, had philosophic views); they were people with remarkable skills in rhetoric and in the ways of argumentation. Through their activities, they did two important things (which Socrates expanded upon): they shifted attention from the "world" and its collective destiny to that of the individual man, and they opened the way to a thorough analysis of our ways of thinking.

In turn, Plato had taken over from Socrates two ideas: that of the permanent character of the concept and the identity between the concept and the external reality ("Words are akin to the matter which they describe," says Timaeus), and expanded upon them in a different, new direction which would ultimately lead to the eternal and abstract Idea. The most famous expression of these ideas is found in the parable of the cave, in Book 7 of *The Republic*. There Plato distinguishes between the world of the contingent reality accessible to us through senses, the *doxa*, and that of the transcendent ideas, accessible only to the true knowledge, *episteme*. Moreover, he accords ontologic status to the two worlds; since the essence of the world of Ideas is superior and different from that open to the senses (the world of "sublunar events"), it is clear that experimentation, for instance, which can be conducted only in this inferior realm, will not be relevant insofar as the "real," the "true" (and as a corollary the "beautiful") are concerned. "I first lay down the theory which I judge to be soundest," says Socrates in *Phaedo*, "and then whatever seems to agree with it—with regard either to causes or to anything else—I assume to be true, and whatever does not, I assume not to be true."[18]

Aristotle differs from Plato, first in the fact that while retaining the distinction between the two ways of knowledge, between *doxa* and *episteme*, he allows the two worlds to interpenetrate: in his view they both belong to ONE existence. Of the two, one represents that which is fixed, constant, unmovable, *the essence, the nature* of the existent, while the other represents the impermanent, the changing and the changeable. *Aristotle is always in search of the nature of the thing (or subject) and its cause.* In the *Metaphysics*, we find the following breakdown of the *episteme* as a body of true knowledge: *episteme* is divided into *praxis, techné,* and *theoria*. In turn, *theoria* is subdivided into the following three domains:

---

[18]*Phaedo,* 100a.

mathematics, physics, and theology. The practical sciences are those dealing with actions following a moral judgment (ethics, politics). *Techné,* sometimes translated as art, sometimes as "applied science" or craft, is used in a different way by Aristotle as compared with Plato. For the latter, *techné* meant "a professional competence as opposed to mere chance,"[19] while for Aristotle "*techné is* a characteristic geared toward production (*poietiké*) rather than action (*praktiké*). It arises from experience (*empeiria*)...and passes from experience to *techné* when the individual experiences are generalized into a knowledge of causes."[20] *Theoria*, which for Plato was the contemplation of the Good, becomes for Aristotle a quasi-divine occupation: it is the search for the apodictic, for the essences, it is the actualization of the potencies lying in reason. For Aristotle, God himself is the absolute theoretician (and this thought has been taken over and infinitely amplified by the monotheistic Middle Ages, be they Christian, Jewish, or Islamic theologies).

This positioning of "physics" as a theoretical endeavor—in the sense he meant "theory"—prevented Aristotle from discovering "laws of nature" as defined by the GN revolution; all he could do was to use empirical observations in combination with logic to establish certain "principles." Many of them were erroneous but this Aristotle wouldn't notice: in some cases he relied too much on the "principle" governing the facts, in others, due to material limitations, he couldn't accurately perform the relevant experiments.[21] For a modern scientist studying, say, motion, Aristotle's basic premise, that of studying "the nature of the motion," is wrong. Moreover, he would consider wrong even the definition of the object of the study: "Nature is a *principle* of motion and change," writes Aristotle.[22] To understand today the origin of this "confusion," we must go back and consider the meaning the word *nature*, (*phûsis*) had for the ancient Greeks. In his *Natural History of Birds*, Buffon pointed out that there are two ways to understand the word *nature*. In its absolute sense it is the *locus* of all the phenomena for which we can observe causal relationships. In modern parlance, this would be the nature around us as we experience it through our senses and understand it in the thinking process, the Nature. The second meaning is

---

[19]For the various meanings of the key terms used here, see, for instance, F.E. Peters, *Greek Philosophical Terms* (New York: New York University Press, 1967), pp. 190-193.
[20]Ibid, p. 191.
[21]Aristotle was not impervious to the need to know accurately—that, is by means of experimentation—the facts, as some people have claimed: "It is for the empirical scientist to know the fact," he wrote in the *Posterior Analytics*; he himself has performed much experimental work in his biological research.
[22]Both quotes are from Book 3 of the *Physics*, 200b15; my emphasis.

that of nature as representing all the qualities bestowed by Nature as defined above, upon humans or animals. The expression *peri phûseos* appears as the title of one of Empedocles' poems and as a generic title of several pre-Socratic works. Hippocrates in his *History of Medicine* (fifth century B.C.) takes issue with doctors influenced in their judgment by those who wrote such *peri phûseos;* it is difficult to establish which of the two senses of the word was adopted by Hippocrates. A well-known translator and commentator of this work, A.J. Festugière, would say, Nature. A no less distinguished specialist, Pierre Hadot, would say that the second meaning is that adopted by Hippocrates. It is easier to decide for the second meaning in Plato's *Phaedo*: there *historia peri phûseos* has clearly the meaning of "the causes for each thing."[23] That is, *phûsis* represents a relationship, a quality, the intrinsic. One can certainly find places were *en tei phûsei* stands for the "intrinsic," the essence of the thing as for instance in *Parmenides*, 132c. This oscillation between the two meanings not only illustrates the difficulties in understanding the ancient Greek texts today, which I alluded to above; it also indicates an evolution, or at least a shift, in the ways of thinking between Plato and Aristotle. The latter would use both meanings, interchangeably, sometimes even simultaneously.[24] In some cases, however, as for instance in the following sentence taken from *On the Heavens*, Aristotle would explicitly use *phûsis* for nature in the absolute sense: "But God and nature create nothing that is pointless."[25]

The discussion concerning the meaning of "nature" and "the principles of the inquiry of nature" as they were developed in Aristotle's works (and not only in the *Physics*) is fascinating and could constitute in itself the subject of a book (in fact, several books have already been written on the subject). This is not my purpose here though; what I would like to make clear here is the fact that the Aristotelian—and

---

[23]*Phaedo*, 96a.
[24]Since Cornford explains this point very clearly, I will quote him: "Aristotle tries to reduce to this pattern even such questions as the cause of an eclipse of the moon. He treats 'eclipse', not as event, following upon some earlier event called its cause, but as an attribute of the moon. The moon is the subject, and when you state the fact that it is eclipsed, you are saying that it has the attribute 'eclipse'. If you then ask for the reason—Why has the moon this attribute?—the answer will be the same as if you ask for a definition of 'eclipse'. 'It is clear', he writes 'that the nature of the thing and the reason of the fact are identical. The question "What is an eclipse?" and the answer: "Privation of the moon's light by the interposition of the earth", are the same as the question: "Why is there an eclipse?" and the answer: "Because of the failure of light when the earth is interposed"'. Thus the inquiry for the cause of an event is reduced to inquiry for a definition of an attribute" (*The Unwritten Philosophy*, p. 88).
[25]*On the Heavens*, 271a32.

The Greek Way to Disciplinarian Thinking

following it, *the entire pre-GN thinking—was nondisciplinarian in the sense in which I define "disciplinarian thinking" in this work*. To conclude this general presentation of the ancient Greek version of disciplinarian thinking, or in other words, the strategy used by classical Greek philosophy to define the objectives of its intellectual pursuits and to achieve "truth," I shall briefly mention the issue of "classification" in Aristotle's works. Plato and the Stoics should also be mentioned, because of their role—together with the crucial role played by Aristotle—in the shaping of medieval thought. They also influenced many of the precursors of the GN revolution and, thus, the onset of *disciplinarian thinking*. First, I must remind the reader that in this context I use the words "science" and "philosophy" interchangeably; in the *Metaphysics*, we read that "all men suppose what is called wisdom to deal with the first causes and the principles of things."[26] The seeker of wisdom, i.e., the philosopher, must seek "universal knowledge," since this is the hardest to achieve. We have to aim at the most difficult things, the most remote from the sensory experience, we must seek "the knowledge of that which is most knowable." "And," continues Aristotle, "the most exact of the sciences are those which deal most with first principles."[27] In Book 4, we find the connection with the "classification": "For 'philosopher' is like 'mathematician'; for mathematics also has parts, and there is a first and second science and other successive ones within the sphere of mathematics."[28] Division is therefore necessary for a better knowledge; moreover, as we have seen above, there is a hierarchy within the different levels of knowledge. Plato has already pointed out in the *Statesman* the need to divide the totality of sciences into two classes, one "applied," the other "pure." At the beginning of Book 6 of the *Metaphysics*, after stating that "natural science, like other sciences...is neither practical nor productive," Aristotle comes to the conclusion that "natural science must be theoretical." Moreover, he clearly defines its object of research: "It will theorize about such being as admits of being moved, and only about that kind of substance which in respect of its formula is for the most part not separable from matter."[29] From here on, the text becomes very difficult to understand; he defines the object of "theoretical science" as that which is "eternal and immovable and separable." But then he makes the distinction between "natural science" which "deals with certain movable things" and the "theoretical" and "first" sciences. He concludes that "there must then be three theoretical

---

[26]*Metaphysics*, 981b25.
[27]Ibid, p. 982a30.
[28]Ibid, p. 1004a5.
[29]Ibid, p. 1025b25.

philosophies, mathematics, natural science,"[30] after which the "divine," the "highest genus," and the "universal" come into play and we are left wondering. It is however clear that we are presented with a hierarchical classification of knowledge, some sort of a disciplinarian division, but this division is determined by *essential qualities* of the objects of our thinking, by *the nature* of the things as discovered by our minds. At the highest level, that of theoretical thinking, the soul is intimately connected with the essential quality of its object; this will not be the case at a lower level of knowledge such as that obtained through sensorial perception. The two ways of knowledge are thus separated epistemologically, not methodologically. Even if we could find here a methodology of scientific endeavor, it would not be the essential criterion for the division among disciplines.

On the other hand—says Aristotle—among different "disciplines" situated at the same level of the above hierarchy, one can use a formal method of inquiry, a logic (*logikos*), based on a clear definition (*logos*) of the object of study. This point is essential to our discussion concerning the possibility of the inter- or transdisciplinarian thinking. "Of propositions or problems there are...three divisions, for some are ethical propositions, some are on natural science, while some are logical."[31] As an example of a logical proposition he gives: "Is the knowledge of opposites the same or not?"(!) What are the "problems" Aristotle talks about? In the same *Topics* we have the answer clearly stated: "A dialectical problem is a subject of inquiry that contributes either to choice and avoidance, or to truth and knowledge, and does that either by itself, or as a help to the solution of some other such problem."[32] Now, "dialectical" is not to be understood in the Platonic sense, since for Plato the dialectic was a technique which helped (re)discover the Ideal Forms, while for Aristotle the object of the first philosophy is the "immovable substance," *ousia*, and "it will belong to this (that is, to the first philosophy) to consider being qua being."[33] Logic seems therefore to be some sort of a "universal tool" equally applicable when dealing with problems related with either physics or ethics. The Stoics have changed the picture insofar as the meaning and the hierarchy of the various disciplines are concerned: for Chrysippus, logic, comprising rhetoric and dialectic, has become the only and the absolute way to certainty and truth. But for the Stoics logic is more than a mere tool, it becomes one of the virtues of the philosopher. *Phûsis*, in its absolute sense, has been

---

[30]Ibid.
[31]*Topics*, 105b20.
[32]Ibid, p. 104b1.
[33]*Metaphysics*, 1026a30.

extended to the entire universe. *Logos* changes meaning again, and becomes at the same time the cosmos, that which has created it and its meaning too. There is a logos of nature (cosmos), one of human nature, and one of the human mind reasoning about the above two. Physics is the study of the first, ethics of the second. *Logic studies the (same) logos, embodied in our ways of knowing.* The essence, the idea, the *ousia* has penetrated everything: the logos brings together the realms separated until this point. Reason understands the sublunar world as well as that of heavenly spheres, because they are penetrated by the same unifying principle which is the logos. This is the great change brought upon by the Stoics, a change which had the potential to lead to the creation of a science of the GN type, if a new development hadn't changed the course of Western history and of its ways of thinking established by the ancient Greeks. This development was the appearance of a new way of thinking based on the fusion between Greek philosophy and Judeo-Christian theology. Even though Clement of Alexandria, Plotinus, and St. Augustine, were aware of the distinctions between the three different ways of seeking the truth represented by Plato, Aristotle, and the Stoics, they all preferred Plato. For the next thousand years, the Christian world was to be dominated by the idea that the only reality worthy of study was God, the Creator and the Redeemer.

3

Western Thinking between the End of the Greek World and the Middle Ages

The end of the Greek world is interwoven with the beginning of Christianity in Europe; we shall have to continue therefore from this point the story of the unfolding of *disciplinarian thinking* I began to tell in the previous chapter. Many wondered why Greek, and later, Hellenistic and Roman, thinking did not produce the tools and the means needed for a scientific revolution. The argument that a society based on slavery did not need to channel knowledge toward the improvement of its material conditions due to the unlimited supply of manpower was often mentioned: "This mischievous separation of the logic from the practice of science was the result of the universal cleavage of society into freeman and slave."[1] History recorded events which seem to confirm such a hypothesis: allegedly, the Roman emperor Vespasianus denied an inventor the right to pursue work on some sort of a mechanical crane. Pertinax seemingly destroyed a device built as a car for public transportation. But I am suspicious of simple arguments when it comes to such complicated things as human minds and social structures; I am afraid that those who claim this explanation were influenced too much by some of Francis Bacon's ideas or by Marx and Engel's dialectical materialism. Unlike classical Greece, which was divided in a multitude of small city-states, the Hellenistic world, and even more so the very extended and the technically minded Roman Empire, could have benefited from technological progress based on the development of science. Still, one cannot argue with the facts: the scientific revolution did not happen at the beginning of the first millennium A.D. Why? The answer may have to do with the social and political conditions of the late Roman world, but in a more intricate way.

---

[1]Farrington, p. 303.

At the beginning of the Christian era, the interpenetration between the two worlds, the Roman and the Greek, was complete: Horace, the poet, wrote in his *Epistles* that as Rome captured Greece militarily, she was conquered in turn culturally by the Greeks. This Greco-Roman age (the period extending roughly from Alexander the Great to the end of the Roman Empire) was a time of cultural symbiosis: "The bilingualism of the Greco-Roman world means that from about 100 B.C. European science had two tongs, but the work was unequally distributed between them. The work of advancing the now traditional branches of science continues to be done in Greek. In Latin was done a work of assimilation and adaptation to Roman needs, which involved criticism selection, and organization, and produced a few masterpieces of a new type."[2] This bilingualism was very important for the development of the later scholastic culture. Many Greek works will be absorbed through Latin translations, and during the first centuries C.E., a significant amount of Greek philosophy was often transformed into something different, if not always into something new, by Roman authors. This "filtering" process is a very interesting one and would merit a discussion in itself. The question is whether a given historical period or a given civilization is characterized by new and specific cultural products generated by this civilization or rather by its "filtering patterns," that is, by the way it absorbs the dominant ideas surrounding it. The question has already been asked in contemporary socio-historical studies.[3] I shall come back to this point when we discuss and try to understand the formation of *disciplinarian thinking* during the tumultuous period between the end of the Middle Ages and the dawn of modernity, roughly between the periods the Italians call *Rinascita* (the times of Dante and Petrarch) and *Rinascimento* (the Renaissance). One can find many important figures who "filtered" and reshaped the classical Greek culture: Galen, the dominant personality of the medical sciences of his time; Varro, with his encyclopedic work *Nine Books of Disciplines;* Cicero; Lucretius, the author of *On the Nature of Things;* the Stoic Seneca; and Plinius the Elder, the author of *Natural History,* are probably the greatest names of this Greco-Roman period. In the narrow context of this work, we can only mention their names; we shall meet them again through the influence they

---

[2]Ibid., p. 246.
[3]I have in mind in particular the works of Ioan P. Couliano. See, for instance, his book *Eros and Magic in the Renaissance* (Chicago and London: University of Chicago Press, 1987).

exercised on other authors at other times, during various phases of the unfolding of story of the birth of *disciplinarian thinking*.[4]

Problematic is also the argument advanced by other authors about the alleged contempt the ancient Greeks had for the "mechanical arts"; Farrington quotes Xenophon as saying that "what are called the mechanical arts carry a social stigma and are rightly dishonored in our cities. For these arts damage the bodies of those who work at them...(and) this physical degeneration results also in deterioration of the soul."[5] It is true that Aristotle claimed that mathematics originated in Egypt because the priestly caste could indulge in a leisurely life, and for Plato, the creator of the material world surrounding us was a *demiourgoi*, a name reserved in Homer for craftsmen, metalworkers, potters, masons, etc. And even if we would agree with Francis Bacon in his *Novum Organon*, that the technical discoveries preceded philosophy in the ancient world, it is difficult to agree with the second part of his statement: "When contemplation and doctrinal science began, the discovery of useful works ceased." Much more interesting and fruitful to our discussion would be the question concerning the place held by experiment and experimentation in classical Greek philosophical thinking. As I pointed out already, Aristotle did not reject the experiment as a means toward knowledge. But what kind of knowledge can be achieved through experimentation is a different question. In Plato we find a "structural" problem; the craftsman "does not make that which really is" because for Plato, that which "really is" should be the Idea. Learning from experiment, any experiment, would yield an inferior or incomplete knowledge. Still in various dialogues we may find statements like "it is beyond the power of human nature to achieve skill without any experience."[6] Experiment begins with observation and should end with a quantitative result, following a measurement. To us today, it seems that nothing is more reliable than a quantitative measurement of something we can observe or produce and reproduce. But time and again, we observe Plato moving in the "right" direction only to find him stop and stumble on the threshold of the quantitative (which is somewhat surprising after Pythagoras). Aristotle, much closer to observation, experimentation, and classification, came at times very close to the modern scientific approach. However, in spite of his departure from Platonic philosophy, he remained a prisoner of "theoretical thinking" as

---

[4] A good brief description of their works and influence can be found in David Lindberg's book *The Beginnings of the Western Science* and, for the period ending with Galen, Farrington's *Greek Science*, already mentioned.
[5] Farrington, p. 28.
[6] *Theaeteus*, 149c.

we have seen in the previous chapter. I will mention only one of the many examples one can find, from the sixth book of the *Physics*. Notice the relation between the "theoretical" and the "experimental" inferences: "And since every magnitude is divisible into magnitudes—for we have shown that it is impossible for anything continuous to be composed of indivisible parts, and every magnitude is continuous—it necessarily follows that the quicker of two things traverses a greater magnitude in equal time, etc."[7] During the post-Aristotelian era, in particular under the influence of Stoic thinking, learning about the material world through direct, sensory experience has become "legitimate." But experimenting is not enough; we must have some guiding ideas for the interpretation of the results. Those used by Aristotle were erroneous. As long as our "guiding ideas" are wrong, the concepts we use will be inappropriate too. It took a thousand years for Western civilization to discover this dialectical relationship between the two. Logical thinking provides a frame in which concepts in terms of which we describe an experiment can be manipulated; however, logic alone cannot complete the picture. The generic concepts used by Aristotle, such as "heavy" vs. "light," "natural and perfect" vs. "imperfect" movement, were in agreement with his ontology rather than with the world as it presented itself to experiment. The Stoics did not do enough, before they disappeared from the scene, to replace the Aristotelian concepts with new ones, in agreement with their ways of approaching things. Could a "Stoic science" have accelerated the way to the GN revolution?

Of course, we should not forget the scientific accomplishments of Archimedes (died 212 B.C.), of Aristarchus of Samos, of Heron of Alexandria, and of Galen, during the first and second centuries of the Christian era. But their works were exceptional; in historical perspective they appear like tiny islands of knowledge in a huge ocean of ignorance. It was not, however, an ignorance caused by lack of understanding; it was rather a willful rejection based on quite rational arguments. A new era has just begun. Tertullian was one of its first heralds when he wrote in his *De Praescriptione Haereticorum* (around 200 C.E.) that after the Gospels, investigation is not needed any longer. He was followed by St. Basil (fourth century C.E.) who wrote "grand phenomena do not strike us the less when we have discovered something of their wonderful mechanism...let us prefer the simplicity of faith to the demonstrations of reason."[8] This new era was one of the fusion between a world still dominated by Greek philosophical thinking and that of the newly born

---

[7] *Physics*, 232a25.
[8] Quoted by Jennifer Trusted in *Physics and Metaphysics* (London and New York: Routledge, 1991), p. 2.

Christianity, a religion originating in monotheistic Judaism. Fusion may be too neutral a word though; this process of fusion was a permanent battle as well. At first, Christianity had to withstand the increased persecution of an evolving pagan-state religion. The cult of the emperor replaced the pluralistic and tolerant attitude of the pre- and early imperial times. Later, when the Roman Empire became Christian, during the reign of Constantine, the nature of the battle changed: the new religion had to be forged into an all-encompassing worldview, able to fight doctrinarian heresies within its body as well as the competition of (the still pagan) philosophy. It is interesting to observe how such varied factors as the political, the psychological, and the philosophical merged to remold ways of thinking developed between Athens and Jerusalem. The world was remodeled in accordance with the structures of the empire: God is the supreme emperor, Almighty but remote from the material world as the emperor is from his people. The earthly emperor becomes the intermediary between the transcendental God and the immanence of everyday, concrete experience. This situation, thought out in philosophical terms, lead to the reappearance of Plato's *demiourgoi* in the new context of a hierarchical monotheism. Soon, the fight against gnosticism was to become a fierce battleground inside Christianity.

We recognize a deep change in the ways of thinking brought forth by Christianity. We have seen that Aristotle considered the search for the *ousia* the highest philosophy; in the new scheme of things, the human spirit, that part of us capable of seeking the absolute, became committed to the search for the divine. But God could only be approached through pious contemplation and not through critical, rational thinking (St. Thomas Aquinas and Maimonides came much later). The early Fathers of the Church were in search of something alive, beyond nature and words, something which exceeded the human ability of comprehension and at the same time was the only worthwhile "object" of contemplation. That was Christ and his words embedded in the Gospels. According to St. John, Christ was identified with the Logos of God. Through *logos* and *pneuma* man was able to reach the proximity of God. We can see how the concepts, the epistemology, and even the ontology of the Greeks were appropriated by the emerging Christian theology. Both Plato and Aristotle were adopted by this new thinking, and during the years of formation and crystallization of scholastic thinking, we shall find them both playing the role of "guiding spirits."

In open-minded Alexandria, which was for centuries the stronghold of Hellenistic philosophical and scientific thinking, Origen (died c. 250 C.E.), the student of Clement, the great opponent of gnosticism, wrote in a letter to a former pupil: "I would like to see you use all your intellectual prowess in the service of Christianity, which must now become your supreme task. To succeed, you must borrow from Greek philosophy all the knowledge which may serve to introduce Christian thinking, all the geometry and astronomy useful to explain the New Testament; study also what philosophers had to say about geometry, music, grammar, rhetoric and astronomy, the auxiliaries of philosophy, as *philosophy itself is an auxiliary of Christian theology.*"[9] These words echo the teachings of his own master, Clement, for whom philosophy was an introduction to the *true gnosis*. Those who practice the gnosis take from every discipline that which is useful for the attainment of the truth, he wrote. However, advised Clement of Alexandria, although the true believer, while attaining the highest degree of belief through gnosis (not gnosticism!), "shall not neglect encyclopedical knowledge and the Greek philosophy, he should not consider them essential."[10] For these early Christian thinkers, the physical world had a rather symbolic existence; it was there to guide men to discover their true essence, the spiritual one. It is important to understand this deep transformation in the ways of thinking brought upon by Christianity. The replacement of nature as the object of rational reflection with the Scriptures represents much more than a narrowing of interests and a "provincialization" of the philosophical endeavor. It was not only the fear of becoming contaminated with impure or unworthy thoughts that pushed the founding fathers of Christian theology and the future scholastic thinking toward exegetic discourse. True, in its inner core, Christianity was an outgrowth of the Judaic monotheism; but once projected through a gigantic mass movement into the endless confines of the pagan world, the newly born religion became theologically structured by the incredibly complex tissue of the Greek-pagan ethos. To fully realize the situation, we must take into account the great changes introduced by the Epicurean, Stoic, and Neoplatonist currents in Greek philosophy. These changes brought an increased awareness of the Self to the spirit of the cultivated pagans of Alexandria, Rome, and Athens. It is true that Socrates made the "know thyself" into the most important activity of the wisdom seeker. But there was an important difference. The most direct way to explain the difference seems to me this: When Socrates spoke about death he was serene. He knew that the soul was immortal. "Anyone," he said in *Phaedo*, "who does not know and cannot prove that the soul is immortal must be afraid, unless he is a fool."[11] Socrates was not a fool and he was not afraid. Three hundred years later, people were

---

[9] From Jean-Yves Leloup, *Introduction aux "Vrais Philosophes"* (Paris: Albin Michel, 1998), p. 35; my emphasis and my translation from French.
[10] Ibid., p. 64.
[11] *Phaedo*, 95d.

afraid of death; they were frightened of the uncertainties carried by the mystery hidden in human existence, scared by the presence of evil in the world. The Stoics taught people that they have a consciousness which is independent and in touch with the purest and highest essence of the world (very much like the God of the monotheistic religions). This discovery brought with it a troubling sense of responsibility. All of a sudden, men became free in the world, and at the same time in some unclear ways prisoners of their own consciousness. Some began to speak of a "spiritual crisis," of an anxiety which reached not only the philosophers but the large masses as well. "People were worried, felt menaced in their souls and their bodies by mysterious powers. The world has been conquered by evil demons who attacked the imagination as well as the body. Moral life resembles more and more a fight between good and evil demons."[12] Gnosis was close.

Parallel with the spread of this diffuse anxiety, theology itself developed into something quite different from what it used to be in the times of Plato and Aristotle: it became a rationalization and a systematization of the religious ideas. The Stoics laid out a list of religious "topics" and the methodology to deal with them; the Neoplatonist philosophers took the process a step further and transposed the discussion from the physical into the metaphysical realm. Hadot, from whom I quoted above, explained very clearly the convergence of the pagan and Christian theologies in the doctrine of the divine hierarchy: For Plotinus, the One, which is to be found at the top of the hierarchy of being, produces the Divine Mind, which in turn produces the Souls. Origen will identify the One with the transcendental God, while the Logos is the second God who imparts the power of unity to the multiplicity of beings. The tracks were very close, and soon, the pagan philosophers who were trying to reach the One through various rituals met the Christian theologians on the common grounds of contemplation and mystical ecstasy. We are told by Porphyry (in *Plotinus' Life*), that when the pious Amelius tried to induce Plotinus to visit a temple, he was answered, "It is not me who has to go to the gods, but the gods should come to me." We are surprised to discover that both St. Augustine and Pseudo-Dionysus did not consider this a licentious answer: they assumed that Plotinus, the pagan, was able to establish a direct relationship with the transcendent God of Christianity. As a result of this process of fusion, the philosophy of the Neoplatonist pagans translated into the transcendental religion of God the One, and Christian theology became the philosophy of the Western world. For almost a thousand

---

[12]From Pierre Hadot, *Encyclopédie de la Pléiade*, vol. 2, *Histoire des Religions* (Paris: Gallimard, 1972), p. 87; my translation.

years, beginning with the third century C.E., a new worldview would slowly build itself up on this basis; it would be a worldview which would deny the reality of the concrete, of the immanent. It would also be essentially statical (in that it resembled the Greek love for the static) and would be dominated by the idea of the union with the transcendental through a special type of knowledge, gnosis. Thus, not only the meanings of concepts and ideas have been channeled into a religious direction, but even the most basic tenet of Greek philosophy, an idea expressed by Plato in *Theaeteus*, that "the sense of wonder is the mark of the philosopher," has been altered. Philosophical reflection was to become contemplation of the Divine. At the most, as St. Augustine put it, "for the Christian, it is enough to believe that the cause of all created things, whether in heaven or on earth, whether visible or invisible, is nothing other than the goodness of the Creator, who is the one and true God."[13]

This "philosophical interregnum," during which Greek and Latin Christian writers and Fathers of the Church met pagan thinkers influenced by exotic oriental religions and esoteric mysticisms, created an impressive chaos of ideas. Out of this, scholastic philosophy will be born. St. Augustine was very much influenced by the Neoplatonists Plotinus and Porphyry; Calcidius, a Christian, transmitted to the Middle Ages Plato's *Timaeus*, and Microbius, probably a pagan, wrote a commentary on Cicero. We have also Iamblichus, Proclus, and Pseudo-Dyonisius, and Boetius with his famous *Consolation of Philosophy*. The reader may ask why these names, which seem far removed from the question of the emergence of modern science, are mentioned here. I want to stress the point, often challenged or neglected, that this period was a very fertile one, not at all a "dark" one, as some like to call it. It was a time of intense intellectual activity, during which new worldviews were forged; in the process, a rigorous systematization of theoretical thinking was achieved. Logic and its tools were developed to their utmost. A new way of reasoning, which will lead to the "phantasmic concepts," emerged. We will discuss in the next chapter the role played by these "phantasmic concepts" in the GN revolution. As physical nature was replaced by Divine Nature, the attribute of "infinity" was transferred to it too; the Greeks did not like this concept, which was leading to paradoxes. The new worldview will incorporate it and when the time comes, this ability to handle paradoxical concepts will serve well Nicholas Cusanus' philosophy based on the ideas of "coincidentia oppositorum" and an infinite universe. This in turn, will make the transition to the Copernican world easier. It is true that religious

---

[13]Quoted by Trusted, p. 4.

dogmatism pushed to extremes sometimes closed certain horizons; on the other hand, it also sharpened certain intellectual faculties and refined thinking habits which, as soon as new doors opened, enabled a very rapid movement toward entirely new ways of thinking. Through its offspring, scholastic philosophy, the period discussed above opened the road to the GN revolution and through it, to *disciplinarian thinking*.

The unstable, "magmatic" situation characteristic of the emerging Christianity was manifest not only in the intellectual realm. The fight between various cults, fractions, and beliefs within the Christian faith had political and social aspects too. As a unified theology was emerging, splinter groups were rejected; the presence of their members in the major centers of the now Christian empire was forbidden. One of these groups was that of the Nestorians who emphasized Christ's human nature; when the church councils of the fifth century rejected their belief, they moved further east and established themselves within the borders of the Persian kingdom. When in 529 C.E. Emperor Justinian closed the academy in Athens, the Persian king Khusraw the First invited its last members to settle in his country. Over the course of a century, a considerable "transfer to the East" of Greek philosophy and science (in particular medical science) took place. Another century later, when the Arab conquest expanded its borders eastward into Persia and India and westward toward North Africa, the intellectual representatives of the new faith of Islam found themselves surrounded by all the wisdom of the classical Greek and Hellenistic world. That is how the process of the Hellenization of Islam began.[14] As a result, during the reign of the famous khalif Harun-al-Rashid and his less (politically) famous son, Al-Mamun, a dynasty of translators (whose founder was Hunayn ibn Ishaq) began the amazing work of translating all the major Greek philosophers into Syriac (a version of Aramic, the lingua franca in the Middle East for more than a thousand years) first, and then into Arabic. (Not only classical Greek works were translated; Hunyan translated into Syriac the Old Testament too.) According to Lindberg in the book quoted, by the year 1000 C.E., almost the entire corpus of Greek medicine, natural philosophy, and mathematical science had been rendered into usable Arabic versions. The importance of these translations for medieval Europe was enormous. In spite of Duhem's claim that Islamic science lacked originality ("the wise men of Mohammedanism were always the more or less faithful disciples of the Greeks") I would like to point out

---

[14]A good but somewhat outdated reference would be De Lacy O'Leary, *How the Greek Science Passed to the Arabs* (London: Routledge and Kegan Paul, 1949); see also the chapter "Science in Islam" and more recent references therein, in Lindberg's book mentioned already.

that the Islamic world was not only a passive repository of Greek wisdom. Over several centuries it played an active role in furthering research and experimentation in the natural sciences, at a time when in Western Europe the early scholastic tradition rejected it. Of course they had their own limitations: Al-Khindi was unapologetic and clear insofar as the need to keep a steady balance between that which the Ancients have said on a subject and that which the Ancients have not fully expressed. "This according to the usage of our Arabic language, the customs of our age, and our own ability," he added.[15] This addition was very significant: the Arab (Islamic) philosophers, astronomers, mathematicians, and chemists had to respect a tradition which distinguished between the traditional learning based on the Koran and any "foreign" wisdom. Since the first was revealed, they had to be constantly on the watch not to come up with discoveries which would contradict traditional wisdom. That was certainly a severe limitation. Still, they kept open the books containing this foreign wisdom, and their minds continued to ponder upon their content. The observational work and the computations of the Muslim astronomers—Copernicus and Kepler quoted the tenth-century Al-Bhatani's works—as well as their work in optics and chemistry, were very important in keeping the torch burning at a time at which it became extinct around them.

The one who seems to have remembered the burning flame during the ninth century was John Scotus Erigena or Eriugena ("scion of Ireland"; not to be confused with Duns Scotus, born 1265). We are a bit surprised to find out that Eriugena, the Neoplatonist who translated not only Pseudo-Dionysius, but also Maxim the Confessor and Gregory of Nyssa, wrote a book entitled *Periphûseon* (*About Nature*), which sounds very Aristotelian (see the discussion of *phûse* in the preceding chapter). In fact it was a confusing (and somewhat confused) theological treatise which was fusing together Platonic, Aristotelian, and biblical themes. Its great merit was, however, in the fact that it reopened the discussion concerning the immanent in Christian theological thinking. The tension between the claim, on one hand, that God is not identical with His created world and, on the other, that at the end of the cycle encompassing creation, fall, redemption by Christ, and finally, resurrection at the end of the times, the world will return to God, lead to a rethinking of the nature of this world. The trend toward "immanentization," recognizable in some of his immediate followers (such as Heiric of Auxerre, his pupil) or thinkers of the twelfth century (Abelard, Gilbert of Poitiers), will find its full expression in Meister Eckhart's mysticism. Lucian Blaga, observed that the German mystic

---

[15]Quoted by Lindberg, p. 176.

always imagined God in a very dynamic and dialectical way, "to the point that his almost pantheistic description has confused modern commentators and induced them into comparing his ideas with those of Brahmanic religion" (Blaga alludes to Rudolf Otto's book *Mysticism East and West*). "This immanent Christian theology led ultimately to a mysticism of nature, to a sacralization of nature, which in turn again gave legitimacy to the renewed research of nature," concludes Blaga in his book *Experiment and the Mathematical Mind*.[16]

Perhaps the most important contribution Eriugena made to mid-scholastic thinking was the reinsertion of Aristotle in the theological discussion. The partial access to his works, the Platonic bent given by the Arab interpreters (mainly Avicenna), some sharp contradictions with tenets of the Christian dogma, all these made the confrontation with the greatest minds of Greek philosophy difficult. The fact that some of the later scholastic thinkers strongly "resonated" with Eriugena may also be due to the appearance on the scene of another important personality: the first and one of the most famous chancellors of Oxford University, Robert Grosseteste, translator and commentator of Aristotle. And following him immediately came Roger Bacon. Today, it is considered that his role as a pioneer on the road to the reinstatement of science to a legitimate position, and its recognition as a valuable and valid intellectual endeavor, has been exaggerated. The fact is, however, that in spite of his exaggerated fear of the Antichrist and suspicious involvement with alchemy (wasn't Newton involved with it too?), Roger Bacon was a strong proponent of learning through experimentation, of the *scientia experimentalis* and the use of mathematics in all sciences. True, he was not a "natural philosopher" in the sense Newton was and perhaps he spent too much time convincing the Franciscan order to which he belonged and the pope that not only was philosophy not harming the faithful, but on the contrary, philosophy has—when properly practiced—the potential to strengthen faith. But this "if properly practiced" had another meaning too. How was science to be practiced properly? What should be the relationship between our understanding of the world and the messages the world sends to us through observation and experimentation? Where lies the truth, in our minds or in the objects we observe? The confusions arising from the seemingly conflicting ideas of the Aristotelian and Platonic elements embedded in scholastic thought were soon to lead to the clash between the "nominalists" and "realists." The first group had the tendency to emphasize the "concrete," the "singular"; William of Ockham argued

---

[16]In Romanian, *Experienta si spiritul matematic* (Bucuresti: Editura Stiintifica, 1969), p. 52; my translation.

that while our mental concepts are universal, our statements can be either true or false because they reflect the nature of the things outside our mind. That brought him into conflict with Aristotle.[17] The "realists" (one has to be careful about this denomination), on the other hand, considered the concept, the idea, as real. In a very rough way, one may say that scholastic thought was dominated by the realist tendency. The call for an experimental science could not be made from a "realist" point of view. Some commentators had the tendency to see in Ockham the demolisher of Thomism, the philosopher who gave the final blow to scholastic idealism and opened the road for the scientific revolution to come. But the road to the Renaissance was still long; William of Ockham was a theologian, as was Roger Bacon. They acted within a quite dogmatic realm, and in spite of everything they tried to find the best arguments in favor of a theological dogma. Both moved within the confines of scholastic thought but they moved far off center. In a state of unstable equilibria such a movement could trigger significant changes. And it did; as an example we may consider the renewed discussion of the concept of *motion*.

Was motion, in the Aristotelian sense, a property of the moving body, a *fluxus formae*, or it was simply a succession of places occupied in space by the moving body at different times, *forma fluens*? To a twentieth-century mind this discussion may seem ridiculous; it was probably already ridiculous after Galileo and if not, it was certainly such after Newton. But to illustrate how far Ockham was from these times, let us consider the question in the context of the battle between nominalism and realism. It will not be too surprising to find that William of Ockham, the nominalist, was a defender of the *forma fluens*. John Buridan, who was his contemporary, had the opposite opinion and defended it in the following way: we observe that the cosmos, or at least its upper spheres, are in rotational movement. This is to be expected, since from ancient times it was agreed that circular movement is the perfect kind of motion. It was also stated by Aristotle that movement must be defined in relation to fixed bodies. But the cosmos is not surrounded by anything, since nothing can be outside it, therefore it cannot move. This however is impossible, because it would imply a limitation of God's omnipotence; therefore the *forma fluens* has to be rejected. On the other hand, argued Buridan, the *fluxus formae* hypothesis must be correct since it doesn't

---

[17] A clear and brief discussion of this point and its relationship with the Platonic theory of the universals, of Aquinas' and Duns Scotus' positions, can be found in John Marenbon, *Later Medieval Philosophy* (London and New York: Routledge, 1991), pp. 171-187.

involve any contradiction: if movement is a quality of the moving object, the cosmos can move even in the absence of anything outside it.

From the battles fought by Tertullian and Origen to the quarrel between nominalists and realists, more than ten centuries passed, and during this time many things changed: the ancient Greek wisdom was first rejected, then lost (although never completely); filtered through Islamic wisdom it was then "reinvented" by Jewish and scholastic theologians of the Middle Ages. As all this happened, man changed, the surrounding world changed, and their relationship changed too. Old issues resurfaced, new questions imposed themselves forcefully. Regardless of the nature of the query, it turned out that new thinking tools had become available. The scholastic rigor had sharpened and formalized to an extreme the logic. The incorporation of the paradox into the Christian dogma (through the doctrine of the Trinity and its consequences) opened new horizons. Whitehead, in his book *Science and the Modern World*, observed that the medieval insistence on the Rationality of God and the belief that every occurrence can be correlated perfectly with its antecedents prepared minds for the scientific thinking of the GN revolution. "My explanation," writes Whitehead, "is that the faith in the possibility of science...is an unconscious derivative from medieval theology."[18] A good example to briefly illustrate this evolution could be the that of a sixteenth-century figure, Domingo de Soto. Educated at the University of Paris in a nominalist environment, de Soto lived and worked most of his life in Spain in a Thomist environment. He spent his entire (intellectual) life between nominalism and realism. When he began, guided by the fourth book of Aristotle's *Physics*, to study the problem of space and motion, this common heritage helped him apply to the real (natural) world the mathematical techniques developed—as pure mathematics—at Oxford University (by the Mertonians). Through his contributions to the "quantification of the movement and the space," de Soto was one of the precursors of Galileo and Newton.[19]

---

[18] Alfred N. Whitehead, *Science and the Modern World* (New York: MacMillan Company, 1946), p. 19.
[19] See William A. Wallace's article on Domingo de Soto in *Hispanic Philosophy in the Age of Discovery*, ed. Kevin White (Washington, D.C.: Catholic University of America Press, 1977), pp. 113-129.

4

The Turning Point

"The Scientific Revolution between 1500 and 1700 was in the first place an intellectual revolution: *it taught men to think differently.*"[1] Since the publication of the book by Bronowski and Mazlish from which I quoted above, many new and different approaches have been proposed for the interpretation of the period covering Renaissance, Reformation, and the scientific revolution (or the "GN revolution" as we call it throughout this book); their common denominator is the belief that, indeed, the West had undergone an intellectual revolution as a result of which we began to think differently. Even the harshest critics of modern Western thought, anchored in the so-called 'traditionalist view'—of whom René Guénon was perhaps the most outspoken representative—acknowledged a deep change in the ways of thinking of Western man during that period. What characterized the change, what are the characteristics of this new way of thinking? In this chapter I will attempt a few answers to these questions, namely, by trying to follow the various roads to this "new thinking," the unfolding of medieval scholastic thinking toward and around this turning point represented by the Renaissance. It will be of course impossible to present a comprehensive picture within the confines of a few pages; each idea discussed here, every personality mentioned, could on their own become subjects of an entire book (and many had been). The list of all the relevant ideas which contributed to the advent of the GN revolution will necessarily be incomplete, and from the gallery of portraits some important ones will be missing. I hope however to be able to render a coherent picture, using a multitude of apparently scattered fragments: when the pieces are all put together, the puzzle should present a reasonable image of the newly born *disciplinary thinking*.

---

[1]Bronowski and Mazlish, *The Western Intellectual Tradition* (New York: Harper Colophon Books, 1960), p. 108; my emphasis.

In an earlier work, *The Common Sense of Science*, Bronowski described the process under discussion as representing a change from a world of things ordered according to their ideal nature, to a world of events running in a steady mechanism of before and after. The "steady mechanism of before and after" is Newtonian mechanical determinism, which describes the movement of material bodies in terms of forces in such a way that changes in position at every moment can be predicted in terms of changes in the acting forces. Two hundred years later, Einstein rethought the basic tenets of Newtonian mechanics and extended them in his theories of relativity,[2] beyond the realm of our sensorial experience. "Before Newton there existed no self-contained system of physical causality which was somehow capable of representing any of the deeper features of the empirical world," wrote Einstein, and he pointed out the importance of the "differential" law (as opposed to the "integral" laws of Kepler and Galileo) which enables us to see "how the state of motion of the system gives rise to that which immediately follows it in time."[3] Einstein emphasized that "only by considering what takes place during an infinitely short time...Newton reached a formulation which applies to all motion whatsoever."[4]

While all agree that the GN or the scientific revolution occurred sometimes during the sixteenth and seventeenth centuries, there is a wide range of ideas relative to the causes of this revolution. Most often we are told that the Renaissance, by rejecting the authority of the Church, reinstated man into a central position through some sort of an anthropological Copernican revolution, a position he lost with the advent of Christianity. The discovery of new continents, the introduction of the printing press, Reformation, the rediscovery of the ancient arts and literature and their dissemination on unprecedented scales were all direct or indirect causes of this radical change. For our purpose it is important to look at changes on a rather "microscopic" scale, the scale on which patterns of thought evolve. After having given some consideration to the origins and the evolution of scholastic thinking in the previous chapter, we would now like to understand, how this metamorphosed

---

[2]One should remember that in fact we have a *special theory* and a *general theory*, and they are distinct theories; because they both contain the word *relativity* and have the same author, people usually clump them together as if there were only one theory, the theory of relativity. For a good, brief, and easy-to-understand recent review, I recommend John Stachel's article in *A Companion to the History of Modern Science*, ed. R.C Olby, G.N. Cantor, J.R.R. Christie, and M.J.S. Hodge (London: Routledge, 1996).
[3]*Ideas and Opinions*, (New York: Laurel Edition, Dell Publishing, 1979), pp. 248-249.
[4]Ibid.

The Turning Point

itself into something totally different, a new way of thinking which led to the GN revolution. Where should we situate the departing point of this process? The authors quoted above came to the conclusion that "the conceptual system of nature which dominated the Middle Ages had been formed...by St. Thomas Aquinas about 1250....The great work of St. Thomas was to join together the system of nature of Aristotle with Christian theology and ethics."[5] Others (Huizinga in his book *Erasmus*, for instance), will agree that St. Thomas had a role to play, but in a paradoxical (and rather negative) way: two hundred years after Aquinas, Erasmus' "revolution" came as a reaction to the limited and limiting views of St. Thomas, as an attempt to reunite the classical world of antiquity with a biblical Christianity. Either way, we notice the link between the Greek and the Christian worlds. Beyond this general statement we are left however to wonder on whose shoulders Galileo, Shakespeare (both born in 1564), and Newton (born in 1642, the year Galileo died) stood. It was claimed that Shakespeare used the physical ideas of the Middle Ages when he made a dying Cleopatra utter the words: "I am Fire and Ayre; my other Elements I give to a baser life"[6] On the other hand, when we read that "the Middle Ages could not have conceived the planets to be made of the same stuff as an apple,"[7] the authors seem to introduce some confusion as to the relationship between the Middle Ages and the GN revolution. (I do not want to add confusion to the confusion, but I believe that, indeed, Shakespeare was also part of the GN revolution!) It is therefore appropriate to ask ourselves: What exactly were "the physical ideas of the Middle Ages"? Did the changes in the ways of thinking we are trying to identify here originate in a detachment and abandoning of old ideas about the world and the generation of new ones, or was the process rather a beating of the old swords (how old were they?) into new ploughs?

When talking about science, we try to "be scientific," that is to use reason only and stay away from such compromising concepts as "magic," for instance. But the role "magical thinking" has played in the birth of the GN revolution cannot be denied (not even played down) in any honest attempt to understand its origins. In a book quoted already in the previous chapter, Ioan P. Couliano discusses at length the "History of Phantasy"; what could phantasy have to do with our discussion? Couliano points out a *continuity* in the relationship between man and the world known to him, at all times, from Greek antiquity through the Middle Ages, and till the dawn of the new era of the scientific revolution.

---

[5]Bronowski and Mazlish, p. 109.
[6]*Antony and Cleopatra* V, 2.
[7]Bronowski and Mazlish, p. 111.

The medium through which this relationship was established and maintained was not material; the connection was mediated through a continuous movement from the individual to the cosmic "pneuma." Above and beyond any other considerations, such as the *purpose* of human existence or the essence of the divinity—dominant ideas from the ancient Greeks to medieval times—the continuity between man and cosmos was established and maintained, according to Couliano, through that strange but extremely significant "object": the spirit, or "pneuma." Aristotle defined the *pneuma* as the mediating apparatus between the soul and the body. It was subtle enough to approximate the immaterial nature of the soul and yet strong, "bodily" enough to withstand the contact with the material. But the same pneuma is the "stuff" the stars are made of. This is the first kind of continuity, let us call it "the inner continuity." Couliano claims another type of continuity too, an "external continuity," which is that of the unbroken relationship between man and his surrounding world, mediated through his imagination. His claim is that not even the dualism introduced by the acknowledgment of the complete separation from the transcendental interrupted this external continuity. The point is a subtle one, but very pertinent to our problem. Since the Transcendental (God in Christianity) is the Creator of the world—through the act of creation He made the chaotic world into a "cosmos"—we humans, created by the same God, are also part of this cosmos. It is therefore reasonable to assume the existence of a permanent relationship between man and his world, and this would not contradict in any way or interfere negatively with the mystical or other attempts to reach the Divine. Magic is the device through which we can reach the pneuma as well as the tool by means of which we can manipulate in and through it. Pneuma is the source of knowledge, magic is the source of power, but the roles can be reversed in this worldview. The power may reside in the pneuma because this is also imagination, and the power of imagination is endless. In any event, it is clear that for the magician—be he a magician such as Giordano Bruno or a Pythagorean astrologer like Kepler—it is completely immaterial what kind of cosmos he considers. To emphasize the fact that the nature or the structure of the cosmos is much less important than the idea of pneuma, Couliano observes that "the Renaissance knows not only one, but at least four types of cosmos: the geocentric and finite cosmos of Aristotle, Ptolemy and St. Thomas; the infinite cosmos of Nicholas of Cusa...; the cosmos of Aristarchus and the Pythagoreans as exemplified by the 'heliostatic' theory of Copernicus; finally, the infinite universe of Giordano Bruno...."[8] The

---

[8]*Eros and Magic in the Renaissance* (Chicago and London: University of Chicago Press, 1987), p. 23.

weight given to "the Copernican revolution" and the simple (and simplistic) linear connection made between Copernicus, Kepler, and Galileo, in establishing the genesis of the GN revolution is, from this point of view, if not wrong, at least irrelevant. We find thus that the road from Copernicus to Newton is not a simple ascent along the path: heliocentrism, Kepler's laws, Galileo Galilei's basic kinematics, Newton's dynamics, followed by the explanation of the movement of planets in the solar system and of heavy bodies on earth. As surprising as it may be, we find in all the protagonists of the scientific revolution a strange—to our minds—mixture of thinking based on experimental evidence combined with quantitative relationships embedded in mathematical laws and, at the same time, ideas belonging to Aristotelian-medieval thinking. Kepler is an "easy target" (astrologer), as Giordano Bruno would also be (alchemist, magician), but Galileo too surprises us. And only because he is able to accurately calculate the geometrical structure of Hell as described in Dante's *Divine Comedy*. Galileo is mostly known through his *Dialogues Concerning the Two Chief World Systems* (1632) and *Dialogues Concerning the Two New Sciences* (1638). In these works we find the probable reason for the fact that he ignored Kepler's elliptical orbit theory: Galileo was still biased, in the most Aristotelian way, toward circular motion. We know that Kepler sent him his book published in 1596, *The Mystery of the Universe* (*Mysterium Cosmographicum*), before he met Tycho Brache in Prague. Galileo was certainly aware of Brache's cosmology, still his hero Salviati, who explicitly says, "I act the part of Copernicus in our arguments and wear his mask," argues only with the Aristotelian-Ptolemaic cosmological scheme. This point has been observed and discussed by many authors who deal with Galileo Galilei.[9] It is interesting in this context to look at some other "strange" ideas expressed by Galileo in his earlier and less frequently quoted work *The Assayer* (1623). Here he discusses the "materiality" of the external world, in particular the question of how to select among the properties of the various objects under study those which should be quantifiable. While he feels compelled to "conceive of any material or corporeal substance...as bounded and possessing this or that shape, as large or small in relationship to some other body...as in motion or at rest," he believes that "tastes, odors, colors, etc....are nothing but mere names for something which resides exclusively in our sensitive body, so that if the perceiving creatures were removed, all of these qualities would be annihilated and abolished from existence." And he concludes: "If ears

---

[9]For a simple and general overview and references, see Michael R. Matthews, *The Scientific Background to Modern Philosophy*, (Indianapolis and Cambridge: Hackett Publishing, 1989).

tongs and noses be taken away, the number, shape, motion of bodies would remain, but not their tastes, sounds and odors." We detect here a vague connection between the four senses and the four elements; and indeed, Galileo goes on to discuss this connection in relation to sight, "the most excellent and noble of all senses," and comes to the conclusion that "it is like light itself."[10]

Let us return to another topic brought up by Couliano, which is also, I believe, very important for our discussion: that related to the role of the *phantasm* in the ways of thinking of these times preceding the GN revolution. Our senses receive messages from the external, corporeal world and these messages have to be conveyed to the soul. The medium which makes the conversion possible is, as we have seen, the *pneuma*. But the actual component of the pneuma which does the transformation is the *phantasia* which "transforms messages from the five senses in phantasms perceptible to the soul."[11] The phantasm becomes thus the basic "thinking unit." That is why, writes Couliano, Kierkegaard said that "pure thought is a phantasm." In his chapter "History of Phantasy" in *Eros and Magic*, Couliano gives a very interesting history of these concepts from Aristotle to Galen and from him through Albert the Great and Aquinas till Ficino and Giordano Bruno. What is significant here is the continuity. The "phantasmic concepts" change from one author to another, but the change is not in their "nature," they remain the appropriate tools to mediate in situations which connect us with the world through our imagination. There is, however, a "bootstrapping" process at work here: the phantasmic concepts are constantly changed in this process of knowing the world through our own phantasms. In his introduction, Couliano writes: "Since the Renaissance, our capacity to work directly with our own phantasms...has diminished. The relationship between the conscious and the unconscious has been deeply altered and our ability to control our own processes of imagination reduced to nothing." With great regret, we must part from Couliano (who was a very interesting and daring mind) with this quotation. To further discuss his claims that magic has many things in common with modern technology, or that Renaissance "science" and modern science are incommensurable, would take us too far from the limited scope of our discussion. However, I will borrow from him the idea of "phantasmic" (and from Aristotle or Chrysippus) in order to make it into that of a *phantasmic concept*. I will claim that the new way to look at the physical world around us was made possible by the introduction of concepts which were not simply generalizations of results of

---

[10]All the quotations in this paragraph are from Matthews, p. 57.
[11]Ibid.

observations or universalization of perceptions more or less common to all rational beings. The new concepts had to have some plasticity, had to be adaptable to a large extent to the requirement to fit mathematical constructs and confirm the self-consistency of sets of laws based on these mathematical constructs. By using the word *phantasmic* I am suggesting the malleability of these concepts, but at the same time, I am stating a continuity between the ways of thinking of the Renaissance "magicians" and the authors of the GN revolution.

Whether or not the fusion of the Greek philosophical tradition with the Christian doctrines occurred in the early Middle Ages, in St. Thomas or Erasmus, it is clear that the process was at work for centuries. The importance of this cultural phenomenon of unprecedented magnitude we call Renaissance in making the transition to the GN revolution has also been abundantly discussed. It seemed a sudden "explosion," a cultural "singularity" having a somewhat mysterious and miraculous character. In trying to understand what happened between the end of the Middle Ages and the onset of the GN revolution, we should start by stating the obvious: during this period, radically new things occurred and new ideas were brought forth. Great expeditions led to the breaking of geographical boundaries and set new horizons. Rebellious movements against the religious establishments, the Reformation—whether it was Luther or Calvin or the Huguenots in France and the Puritans in England—expanded the confines of religious belief and practice far beyond those of the Catholic tradition. It became easier, more in tune with the times, to be rebellious in any endeavor, religious or scientific, philosophical or social. On the other hand, *unity* was sought in order to balance the centrifugal forces at work. I mentioned above the unity through the common soul, the pneuma; another kind of unity was assumed in the two most important political works of this period: Machiavelli's *Prince* and Thomas More's *Utopia*. Both shared a belief in the unity of human nature. At first glance we may think that the two works are very different. One dwelled upon "what men do and not what they ought to do," as Francis Bacon put it. The other, as witnessed to by its title, was a description of a utopian society. Nevertheless, both were rational and pragmatic in their dealing with human reality; that is to say that the man-made social structures are subject to experiment and change, in accord with rationally devised laws. That is what Bacon loved in Machiavelli; it is this kind of empiricism that John Locke will borrow later from Thomas More. An intellectual fever was permeating all fields of knowledge during this period, everywhere loomed a "revolution." Small or of ample proportions, the revolution was to be found everywhere. It is interesting perhaps to observe that during this period the meaning of the word *revolution* has changed from that describing a uniform circular movement around a fixed point (Copernicus' book was entitled *Revolutions of the Heavenly Bodies*) to one describing a radical departure from a well-established state or point of view!

It is true that during this same time, people were burnt at the stake and whole communities were savagely persecuted or even destroyed; we remember the fate of Giordano Bruno and Servetus and St. Bartholomew's night. Some were frightened into silence; and our hero himself, Galileo Galilei, was the most famous among them. Still, fear of persecution didn't prevent Milton from coming to Florence to meet him in 1638. Montaigne was arrested in Paris and Descartes was cautious and went as far as he could to find safety. It is amazing to see how uncompromisingly independent were all these bright minds in spite of the dangers. No fear of earthy or even divine authority could prevent them from proceeding on the paths they had chosen to seek wisdom and knowledge. In the long run they would only be limited by the walls they themselves setup in the process, walls built up by the very method they used, the walls of disciplinarian thinking.

"Le but de nostre carrière, c'est la mort," wrote Montaigne. To make such a statement seems very daring in a France which had just finished consolidating the dominance of the Catholic Church and was preparing to fight the Reformation. Michel Eyquem de Montaigne was born in 1533 and died at the same (Montaigne) castle where he was born, in 1592. He greatly influenced both Descartes and Pascal,[12] who in turn played a very important role in the transition to modernity. They are all important to our story, that of the birth of disciplinarian thinking. But before we go further we must ask: Who influenced Montaigne? I believe that more than by the Reform and the Gnostic traditions of the south of France, he was influenced by the "spirit of Padua." His skepticism could not have originated in Reform, even if this movement had a "revolutionary" character and confronted the basic tenets of the Christian (Catholic) truths; Luther was not a true believer in reason. On the contrary, see, for instance, Shestov on that point (in *Potestas Clavium*). Skepticism is rooted in reason, it is an offspring of reason. And reason meant Greek philosophy. The early scholastic civilization (since a civilization it was!) had rather weak connections with the Greeks: Plato was little known. (Apparently during the early Middle Ages only incomplete fragments of *Timaeus* were available; later Henry Aristippus translated *Phaedo* and *Meno* into Latin in Sicily.) Aristotle was better known: his works on logic were known, but his philosophical works were rediscovered only by the mid-twelfth century. A few poor translations of Homer were also

---

[12]The best book on this subject is written in French: Leon Brunschvicq, *Descartes et Pascal lecteurs de Montaigne* (Neuchatel: Ed. de la Baconnière, 1945).

available. Learned monks occasionally read some of the Roman philosophers and poets: Vergilius and Ovidius, Titus-Livius and Cicero. And we always have to remember the influence of the Muslim and Jewish thinkers: Avicena, Avicebron (Ibn Gvirol), Averroes, and Maimonides, who all, in addition to their commentaries on Aristotle's works, wrote important philosophical and theological works of their own.[13] Things began to change toward the end of the thirteenth century and the beginning of the fourteenth, with Petrarch, Boccacio, and Caluccio Salutati. They were the ones who unearthed the "lost" writings of the ancient Greeks and Romans and made them available, first to their immediate vicinity, that is, to the city of Florence (we should remember that the movement we call humanism was a local, Florentine phenomenon in the beginning), then to all of Italy and through it, to Europe. Toward the beginning of the fifteenth century however, the Church started to look askance at some of the prominent members of the Florentine aristocracy. Under the spell of the renewal, they began to sound heretic. But in fact the humanists were not heretics. Marsilo Ficino did not use the newly discovered philosophy to attack the Church; for him the ancient wisdom of the Greeks just confirmed and reinforced the Christian faith. This point is often misunderstood, I feel: the humanism of the *Quattrocento* was not the source of the new skepticism, that of Montaigne, that which is at the root of modernity. Its real generator was, as I mentioned, "the spirit of Padua."

To understand the birth of this "spirit of Padua" we have, in turn, to go back and look at a development which occurred at and around the university established in 1220 in this city. The University of Padua was one of the first universities established in Europe; the others were those of Bologna, Paris, and Oxford (established at the beginning of the thirteenth century). The birth of the universities, unions of scholars and students (*universitas magistrorum et scholarium*), is related to the expansion of the cathedral schools into larger institutions of learning, built upon the model set by the medieval guild structure. A university would be composed of four faculties, three "superior" (graduate) ones in which cannonic law, medicine, and theology were taught, and an undergraduate one—by far the most populated—in which liberal arts were taught. It is interesting to point out two organizational-structural characteristics which made a certain internal freedom possible in these institutions of higher learning: they were (at least in the beginning) directly under papal or royal authority, and their affairs were run by the teachers (in Bologna by the students) under the leadership of the rector

---

[13]J. Marenbon, *Later Medieval Philosophy* (London: Routledge and Kegan Paul, 1987).

of the faculty of liberal arts (elected by faculty for a limited term). Freedom from local authorities did not necessarily imply freedom of thought (as they were more interested in jurisdiction and taxation). The papal legate, while taking the side of the universities in their quarrel with the local authorities, would interfere in matters of curriculum to a quite substantial extent. For instance, in Paris, in 1215, Robert of Courçon forbade the study of Aristotle's *Metaphysics* and the *Libri Naturales* (the books on physics, cosmology, and biology). But the interdiction was not to last for too long; Roger Bacon, while in Paris between 1240 and 1247, taught in addition to the *Metaphysics*, *Physics* and *De Anima* at the university. And by the mid-century the Arab and Jewish philosophers were studied in the European universities in addition to the Greek.

We have mentioned already the importance of Avicenna; but in connection with Padua, more important was Averroes. During the thirteenth century Averroes was often mentioned as the proponent of the idea that the active intellect is contained in the individual human soul. This was a very important issue for medieval Christian theological thinking (since, as we have seen, philosophy had become the handmaiden of theology, I assume automatically that it was also an important philosophical issue, therefore relevant to our discussion). We have mentioned already the special role granted by Aristotle to the soul: the cosmic *nous* is the unmoved mover, the immortal, unchanging principle of the universe. In medieval theological-philosophical parlance this was synonymous with God. We should remember that for St. Thomas, intellect is identical with the "thinking soul." Aquinas felt he had to discuss at length the relationship between soul and matter not only because Aristotle's discussion may have been contaminated by residuals of pagan thought, but simply because the issue as presented in the *De Anima* was somewhat unclear. Briefly, the argument goes somewhat like this: It is easy to understand the relationship between potency and act. A tree exists potentially in its seed, which obviously is not a tree. It is only potentially a tree. In the same context we understand the relationship between matter and form. Matter is potentially *that*-thing which once endowed with form, becomes *some*-thing. Matter without form is *no*-thing. That is "nothing." A body which has a soul is a living thing. But it has to be a body which has the capacity to be alive. It has a disposition toward something, a *hexis* or *habitus*, as the scholastics would call it. This can be a passive property such as the ability to think, which may be seen as a passive or potential intellect, which in turn, can be activated, thus to become the active intellect. With all these in mind, let us read a fragment from Chapter 5, of Book 3 of *De Anima*:

"Since just as in the whole of nature there is something which is matter to each kind of things...while on the other hand there is something

The Turning Point 53

which is their cause and is productive by producing them all...so there must also be these differences in the soul. And there is an intellect which is of this kind by becoming all things, and there is another which is so by producing all things...and this intellect is distinct, unaffected and unmixed, being in essence activity...and this alone is immortal and eternal."[14] Averroes, in translating Aristotle, added to the confusion by distinguishing between three intellects: "'one which is made 'everything,' one which 'makes all thinking' (*facit ipsum intelligere omne*) and one which 'knows (*intelligit*) all things.'" That which is "made everything," and can be an object of the thought (*res intellecta*) can exist only in a body which is alive, has a soul. But that very same thing "makes all the thinking," is an active intellect and this active intellect is contained in the individual soul. We have closed the circle.

During the second part of the thirteenth century, Averroes was interpreted as saying that the potential intellect is one for all men.[15] Petrarch already attacked the Venetian followers of Averroes, but it was Marsilo Ficino who later complained about the world of the learned being divided in two camps, that of the followers of Averroes and those who follow Alexander of Aphrodisias. Both groups have abandoned any religious thinking, complains Ficino. One group claims the oneness of the human intellect while the individual soul is assumed to be mortal. The others claim that the soul simply vanishes at the death of the body. Pomponazzi, the famous Paduan professor, in a treatise on the immortality of the soul (*De Immortalitate Animae*, 1516), interpreted Averroes as saying that while the intellect common to all men is immortal, this does not confer immortality upon the individual souls. Pomponazzi himself was not convinced; although he doubted the immortality of the souls, he considered the question unsolvable. The university was founded in Padua toward the end of the thirteenth century. At first, its professors came from Paris and the first famous one, admired by Dante and Giotto, was Pietro d'Albano. He was the one who introduced the writings of Averroes, and being overzealous in promoting him and his ideas—some of which had been strongly refuted by St. Thomas and Albert the Great—was suspected of heresy; luckily, he died (in 1303) as the Inquisition was preparing a trial. The pope Eugene IV granted the Paduan university privileges and equal status with the greatest institutions of higher learning in Europe: Paris, Oxford, and Salamanca. After a century of quiet (in spite of a strong neo-peripatetic bias in teaching), with teachers famous but not out of the ordinary, such as Paul of Venice or fra Urbano, the coming of Pietro Pomponazzi to the

---

[14]*De Anima*, 430a10-25.
[15]For a more detailed discussion of this point, see Marenbon, pp. 106-108.

chair of philosophy in 1488 was to make Padua, at least for a while, into one of the centers of free thinking in Europe. Both Bernardino Telesio and Francesco Patrizzi, whom I will mention later, studied in Padua; Giordano Bruno was there too. Of course, Galileo Galilei was to become the most famous professor at this university.[16] Pomponazzi was an Aristotelian (he too!) and to a large extent a scholastic (still) insofar as his style and method were concerned. But he was a free thinker who established a tradition. Toward the mid-fifteenth century, the university in Padua was geared toward humanistic studies, *studia humanitatis*. The main subjects taught were grammar, rhetoric, poetry, history, and moral philosophy. (Basically the disciplines of the "trivium" were conserved, but the "quadrivium" was replaced with new disciplines; I will come back to the meaning of this change in the structure of the *universitas scientiarum*). When French students, attracted by the fame of the Paduan university (and bothered by the political situation at home) went there to study, they discovered that the professors of philosophy not only taught unorthodox things in philosophy, they also taught "poetry": Montaigne mentions in the *Apology of Raimond Sebond* that by 1531, a professor of literature named d'Egnazio was writing a commentary on the seventh chapter of Plinius' *Natural History*, a chapter full of negatives and bitter reflections upon human nature. Of those we find quite a few in Montaigne's essays. It is important however to point out his skepticism, because it will be this skepticism developed by Montaigne which will become a tool for Descartes. Before continuing with Descartes though, let us ponder for a moment this long detour, back to medieval philosophy and from it to "the spirit of Padua." The ancient "pneuma" had been transformed by Christian theology into the problem of the immortality of the soul. We briefly followed its course from Aristotle to Averroes and from his early medieval interpreters to Pomponazzi. My aim was to bring forth the significance of the metamorphosis of an important theological principle—the immortality of the soul—into a secular attitude toward death. In the process, as a by-product, skepticism was rediscovered. But now, under the changed circumstances of the post-Renaissance world, its tools could be applied much more efficiently than in ancient times to intellectual enterprise. "The spirit of Padua" is synonymous with this "new skepticism." Through Montaigne, Francis Bacon, and Descartes, through Spinoza and Leibnitz, it has paved the way to the GN revolution. It follows that the above-mentioned authors are the founding fathers of *disciplinarian thinking*.

---

[16]A brief and interesting presentation of these thinkers can be found in Paul O. Kristeller, *Eight Philosophers of the Italian Renaissance* (Stanford: Stanford University Press, 1964).

The Turning Point

Why is Descartes important to our discussion? First, because he was a self-confessed interdisciplinarian and a practitioner of the "new way" in scientific research. That is, he used mathematics in conjunction with "phantasmic concepts," concepts tailored to be used in mathematical constructs.[17] In letters to Mersenne (1638 and 1640) he wrote, "My physics is nothing but geometry," and "I reduced physics to laws of mathematics." And in the preface to the *Principles of Philosophy*, published in 1644, we read: "Thus the whole of philosophy is like a tree, of which metaphysics forms the roots and physics the trunk, while the branches which grow from this trunk constitute all the other sciences which may be reduced to three: medicine, mechanics and ethics...."[18]

More important, however, is Descartes's "positive skepticism"; I call it positive, because unlike that of the Greek skeptics or even that of his compatriot Michel de Montaigne (whose underlying question was always "Que scay-je?"—What do I know?), Descartes used skepticism to "clean the table in order to make place for those clear and distinct ideas which became his 'operational concepts.' Early in his life, after having studied everything he could find in the books, he was "hampered by so many doubts and errors that the only benefit of my efforts to become an educated person seemed to be the increasing discovery of my own ignorance."[19] As a result, he decided to reform his own ideas and reconstruct them on new foundations. He believed that this was possible because every human being possesses "good sense" or reason, and this, when applied correctly to any object of study, shall lead him to truth. The only trouble is that "we think in different ways and do not fix our attention upon the same objects."[20] In the *Discourse on Method*, he outlined four rules of reasoning and the same number of maxims which guided him in life; for clear reasoning requires clear moral principles to live by. This combination between a permanent and, at the same time, constructive doubt and the affirmation of the "fragmentation" of knowledge—in the sense that one can arrive at truth individually, outside a traditional way of thinking—is, I believe, more important than

---

[17]"Acceleration" would be one of the early "phantasmic concepts" used in kinematics. While velocity is a concept easily arrived at through experimentation and logical reflection (though not the concept of "constant velocity," which cannot be inferred from experiment), acceleration is more difficult. In particular, its relationship with force is not intuitive. Another concept in the early physics which had to be constructed and was not a direct generalization of experience is "momentum." These concepts in the creation of which an intellectual (and sometimes imaginative) effort is required are "phantasmic concepts."
[18]In *Discourse on Method* (London: Penguin Books, 1969), p. 183.
[19]Ibid., p. 38.
[20]Ibid., p. 36.

the famous "cogito ergo sum" which has preoccupied the philosophers and the historians of philosophy so much since it has been uttered. Descartes gave legitimacy to the radicalization of disciplinarian thinking through his rejection of medieval Aristotelianism and the strong dependence of Renaissance men upon the classical world.

This is on the surface. This is what we read in most of the books dealing with the "scientific revolution" as a follow-up of the Renaissance. In fact things are much more complicated: Descartes himself is a more complex character than suspected at first, with his Rosecrucian connections, with his belief in the transcendental ego and in the celestial things which can reach us only through symbols (not too clear or distinct!). We are left puzzled by a thought such as the following one extracted from *Cogitationes Privatae*: "It may seem strange to conclude that some profound thoughts are found in the works of poets rather than in those of philosophers"; and he infers that *"poetae per enthusiasmum et vim imaginationis scripsere"* (poets write [moved by] enthusiasm and the force of imagination). Was he referring to the French "scientific poetry" of the sixteenth century? A glance in this direction is not sufficient to clarify matters. In 1555 Jacques Peletier du Mans published *L'Amour des amours*, the first in a long series of strange literary productions we may call "scientific poetry." He was a contemporary, in France, of Cardan (1501-1576), Montaigne (1533-1592), and Bernard Palissy (died 1590). This entire movement was an outgrowth of the Italian humanism of the Quattrocento; in the best tradition of Ficino and Pico della Mirandola, the French authors of the so-called *Pléiade* tried to organize all the branches of knowledge under the banner of a Neoplatonic mystic knowledge with strong theological undertones. It was an exaltation of the sentiment of being through science, as somebody put it. Mathematics had an important role to play, but in a very peculiar way: it was not the need to associate mathematics with empirical knowledge in order to make it more reliable or more comprehensible. More in line with a Pythagorean tradition mathematics had to help the searching soul to reach this pure God of the intellectual mystics born in the shadow of the Florentine Academy.

In the *Symposium*, Plato talks about "the beauty of laws and institutions"[21]; Diotima tells Socrates that "the candidate for initiation" after having discovered that "nearly every kind of beauty is akin to every other...his attention should be diverted from the institutions to the sciences, so that he may know the beauty of every kind of knowledge."[22] The various scientific domains are united through the common

---

[21]*Symposium*, 210c.
[22]Ibid.

underlying principle of beauty. Ultimately, he who seeks wisdom, the philosopher, "will come upon one single form of knowledge, the knowledge of the beauty...."[23] Peletier follows Plato, and so do most of the authors of the French "scientific poetry" movement. However, when we look at the "substance" of Peletier's "science," it sounds much more Aristotelian. La Boderie's verses too remind one of Aristotle's *Physics*. Still, in both cases, as in many others, Nature is that of the intelligent Creator, the Christian God. It is the same in Ficino, the same in Pico della Mirandola.

However, in a later work of Peletier, *La Savoye* (1572), we find clearly expressed one of the unmistakable signs of the new scientific thinking: the rendering of the facts of our "sublunar" world, strictly based on unbiased observation. In the upper spheres, the stars (moved by God) are still determining our fate; Peletier, even though rigorously deterministic in his thinking, is still far from making explicit the "natural law" at work in the entire universe. (Therefore Einstein's remark concerning the lack of "causal thinking," quoted at the beginning of this chapter, is only partially correct.) In his last work, *Oeuvres poétiques intituleez louanges* (1581), we find *Louange de la science*, a summary of Peletier's views on natural sciences: a review of his day's cosmologies (he accepts the Copernican view: "E méme jusqu'ici à eté crù des Vieus/La Terre étre immobile, et se mouvoèr les Cieus:/ Opinion, qui ét d'autant moins soutenable, etc."), an inventory of unexplained things, an attempt toward a theory of knowledge. He is trying to rid himself of speculations and preconceived ideas; he believes that we learn from practice and practice what we thus learnt: If we are cold and suffer from it, before speculating about causes and effects, we shall build shelters. In many ways he is very close to Francis Bacon, his contemporary (of whom he probably never heard). In many instances he reminds us of Montaigne; and sometimes his old French may convey a surprisingly modern message: "Toe, Un, Tout, Infini, toe le Cercle et le Cantre/ Dont toute ligne sort, où toute ligne r'antre."

The most important poet of the French Renaissance was Pierre de Ronsard. To some extent he belongs to this group of "scientific poets." He was influenced by the Latin poets, Vergilius, Horatius, Lucretius, and the great Italians Dante and Petrarca; he was very much like the Florentine humanists, a believer who worshipped a cosmic harmony imposed by a God who is identified with the Law. In that respect he may have moved a step further than Peletier, toward the "natural law" as defined by the GN revolution. But even if Descartes was impressed by this kind of poetry, it is difficult to find direct connections to their

---

[23]Ibid., 210d.

Quattrocentian roots. Although the "school of Padua" was affected by the Florentine humanist, I stressed already the fact that they filtered it, and made into a positive skepticism. As we have seen, it is in this direction that Descartes moved. As if he wanted to confirm this idea, he wrote that he knew enough about the false science not to run the risk of being duped by the promises of the alchemist, the predictions of the astrologer, the impostures of the magician.

Descartes also stands on the broad shoulders of other "new skeptics," most of whom are much lesser known than Montaigne. Cornelius Agrippa von Nettesheim published in Cologne in 1527 *De Incertitudine et Vanitate Scientiarum*: by the second half of the sixteenth century, there were many freethinkers in France who doubted the immortality of the soul, Providence, even God. Thus, for instance, in 1565 the *Dialogues non moins profitable que facetieux* by Jacques Tahureau were published. The character representing the author (the dialogue was a very much used literary device during the Renaissance years) thanks nature for having blessed him with "this sincerity of the spirit which doesn't give in to an infinity of foolish ideas and irrational facts. There are so many stupid minds around who would rather credulously believe the most untrue things, not willing to judge by reason...."[24] Tahureau did not respect anybody, neither Aristotle nor Plato, Erasmus or Cardan; he was defiant toward any authority.

There is one more figure we must briefly consider in this chapter which tries to present "the turning point" toward the GN revolution and the onset of disciplinarian thinking. This is Francis Bacon. Indeed, isn't he the one who wrote in his *Novum Organum* "that great and solemn debates between learned man often end in arguments over words and names, when it would be more prudent, as the careful mathematicians do, to begin with them and, through definitions, bring the debates to order"?[25] Before Descartes, he criticized the state of the art of "human understanding": "Just as the sciences we now have are of no use in discovering works, so the logic we now have is of no use in discovering sciences,"[26] and added, "for the sciences we now have are nothing more than nice arrangements of things already discovered, not methods of discovery or pointers to new works."[27] What was needed, according to Bacon, were *methods of discovery* and *pointers to new works*. And those could be achieved by connecting the research with mathematics: "*The*

---

[24]From R. Morcay and A. Muller, *La Renaissance* (Paris: del Duca, 1960), p. 420; my translation from French.
[25]*Novum Organum* (Chicago and La Salle: Open Court, 1994), 1:59.
[26]Ibid., 1:11.
[27]Ibid., 1:9.

study of nature proceeds best when physics is bounded by mathematics."[28] This point, the introduction of the idea of mathematization in connection with the method and the need for "pointers," is often overlooked when the role played by Bacon in the emergence of modern scientific thinking is considered. Certainly, his request than one should go back to the down-to-earth facts, to experiment and the accurate description of facts based on observation is recognized; he states it so often and in so many ways in his writings (and not only in the *Novum Organum*) that it could not be missed. But Bacon is more than a proponent of the experimental method in natural philosophy, he is also a precursor of *disciplinarian thinking* in the sense I define it here.

What was that method "hard to practice but easy to explain" Bacon laid out in his *Novum Organum*? To begin with, he gave up the strife for certainty; he wanted to begin with the observation—through senses—but he rejected simplistic conclusions based on sensorial perception only. Instead, he proposed a "new and certain road for the mind to take."[29] A set of rules (methodology) had to be found, so that "the mind is not left to itself, but is always subject to rule";[30] but this methodology has to be based upon concepts which are as adapted to it as are the tools used in mechanical works: "If men had attempted mechanical tasks, using their bare hands alone, without the powerful assistance of instruments, *in the way that they have not hesitated to handle intellectual tasks with bare force of mind*, their achievements would have been small indeed, however strenuously they all labored together."[31] The direction was then set: a new method is to be found and the concepts used have to be appropriate to this new method. Even though these concepts have to be related to sensory observation and the interpretation of experimental data, they must not be crude inferences based only on the generalization and the abstraction of the empirical. They had to be adaptable to *the method*, they must become its *instruments* and *machines*.

Moreover, in order to emphasize the novelty of his approach, Bacon refuses to take issue with the old ways of thinking *on their own ground*; he concedes that they may have some value in "providing employment for professors and benefits for civic affairs." Instead he proposes to assume two parallel ways, one he will call the "Anticipation of the Mind" and the other, the "Interpretation of Nature": "Let there be one method for the *cultivation* of knowledge, and one for its *discovery*."[32] The second is to

---

[28]Ibid., 2:8; my emphasis.
[29]See the preface to *Novum Organum*.
[30]Ibid., 1:38.
[31]Ibid.; my emphasis.
[32]Ibid., 1:40; my emphasis.

become the *disciplinarian thinking* characteristic of the scientific approach in natural philosophy. The basis of the new approach to the interpretation of nature is a new approach toward the basic notions used in the research: "If the notions are muddled and carelessly derived from things, the whole superstructure is shaky," writes Francis Bacon and concludes that most of the notions in use in the description of nature and natural phenomena—among them many taken from Aristotle's *Physics*—are "ill defined and fantastical."[33] For Bacon there were therefore two approaches to the "truths" the human mind sought; it is not sufficiently recognized, that even though he favored the study of nature (he lived already in a world where man had become at the same time its *servant* and its *interpreter* and was preparing the grounds for becoming its *master*), he was aware of the importance of those sciences "based on supposition and opinion." How could have it been otherwise for a man who spent most of his life in the service of the Court of England?

---

[33]Ibid., 1:46.

5

Why Did the Far East Not Have Its Scientific Revolution?

When asked how he explained the miracle of the appearance of modern science in the West, Einstein replied that the miracle is not that science appeared at a certain time in a given place, but that it appeared at all. We have discussed the appearance of a Western science anchored in the GN revolution. The peculiarity of this momentous change in the ways of thinking in the realm of the Greek and Judeo-Christian world is further accentuated by the lack of a similar development in the Far East. This is not the place to discuss the ancient wisdom of India and China. Persia, a buffer between the two worlds, influenced the West certainly and Japan was influenced by the two giants of the Orient. In the geographic realm of the monsoon (I use this metaphor because there were thinkers who granted an exceeding importance to the monsoon in shaping the thinking of the Far East), great religions, philosophies, arts and literature, logic, and mathematical thinking were born and thrived over millennia. Still, a scientific revolution such as that witnessed by the West did not occur in the modern Far East (I use terminology consistent with divisions belonging to our Western culture; I am perfectly aware, however, as the reader should also be, that each civilization has its own ways to divide history and to decide at which stage of development it finds itself at any given moment). One cannot help wondering, why any of these great civilizations did not show inclinations toward the development of an "objective" science of nature. Was it some sort of a "fatality," or a result of a historical "accident"? Was the time not ripe? Or is the fact in some way imbedded in the characteristics of the Eastern "ways of thinking"? And if so, which would these "ways of thinking" be, and how would they differ from those typical of Western thought?

The above questions have often been asked; it is indeed surprising that a culture such as the one that developed prior to Buddhism in India, or later by a cultural environment which made possible the logic of Nagarjuna, did not trigger scientific preoccupations similar to those evolving in postmedieval Europe. The Chinese, who were far in advance of the Europeans at the turn of the first millennium C.E., stopped on the threshold of the scientific revolution. The Japanese, after having rejected the West in the sixteenth century, and having closed the gates of the country to (almost) any foreign influence, seemed to be totally unable to "think scientifically." In the context of our discussion here, these puzzling facts acquire a significance beyond the purely academic: the adoption of modern scientific thinking—otherwise very efficiently absorbed by all these Far Eastern cultures in the last century—may represent only a "surface phenomenon." In their depths, these cultures might still be in a "transient" phase. After having assimilated the scientific revolution of the West, they may still develop in directions different from those adopted by the West. And under certain conditions, this may be a comforting thought.

A Japanese author, Masao Watanabe, wrote that "the scientific approach to nature grew out of the European conception of nature. It would certainly not have arisen in Japan."[1] The core of the argument, used in fact by many in the West as well, is that Western man had built for himself a world in which he stood apart from nature, and this view thus "objectifies" nature, makes it into an external object of dispassionate contemplation. From here to science there is only one step left. On the contrary, in the Oriental traditions (the author refers to the Japanese and Chinese ones), man is part of nature. As a result, he cannot be a dispassionate, external observer of it. Moreover, Watanabe quotes the sociologist Shimizu Ikutaro as saying that the Japanese saw in the merging with a *beautiful* nature the way to protect themselves against the *destructive* character of nature. Indeed, in Japan we often find tenderness when nature is spoken of; take for instance this haiku: "A morning glory took my dipping bucket/I went to my neighbor for water." Or another one by Basho (seventeenth century): "When I look carefully/I see the nazuna blooming/By the hedge." Erich Fromm has discussed the difference between the *to be* cultures and those who emphasize the *to have*. With respect to nature, ours is certainly a "to have" approach. How deep this approach has penetrated our minds seems to be illustrated by this quote from Tennyson: "Flower in the crannied wall,/I pluck you out of the crannies,/I hold you here, root and all, in my hand/Little flower-but *if* I could understand/What you are, root and all, and all in all,/I

---

[1]Masao Watanabe, *The Japanese and Western Science* (Philadelphia: University of Pennsylvania Press, 1976), p. 99.

should know what God and man is."² The poet wants to *understand* nature and through it, to understand himself and God. His first step though is *to pluck* the flower, to make it into an object in order to study it. The Japanese poet, on the other hand, would not even consider touching the "morning glory," he would rather go over to the neighbor's house to get a bucket of water. Basho, when he sees the flower, leans over and "looks carefully." Nature is not an object of study; it is a companion: "Winter moon, coming from the clouds,/to keep me company,/Is the wind piercing, the snow cold?," writes Myoe. Daisetz Suzuki made the same observation when he mentioned both Basho and Tennyson and concluded sharply: "Basho knew better than Tennyson....He realized that the herb was no other than himself."³ Max Weber would have said that Tennyson already lives in a world of *Entzauberung*, of *disenchantment*, in a universe from which the magic has disappeared, in a world in which man observes impartially the absolute laws introduced by God (or nature) to make it turn around.

We cannot tell if Basho "knew better" than Tennyson. In postmodernist terms such a statement does not even make sense. He certainly knew differently. But when Suzuki says "knew better," he has in mind an altogether different meaning of the word "knowledge." In his very popular book, *Zen and Japanese Culture*, Suzuki discusses another haiku by Buson (eighteenth century): "On the temple bell/Perching, sleeps/The butterfly, oh!" The interpretation is based on the same argument referring to the lack of scientific bent in the Japanese mind: the tired butterfly lands on the bell and rests. The fact that the bell may be struck by a monk announcing the prayer does not occur to the butterfly. He lacks "the little 'science' we are so proud of...[and which] makes us conscious of all kinds of uncertainties surrounding us and urges us to dispel them by means of observation, measurement, experiment, abstraction, systematization, etc."⁴ When the frightening sound hits the butterfly, he will take off and move on. He will not "think" that he has miscalculated, he will not be taken aback by the deafening noise which came upon him unexpectedly, remarks Suzuki. He will simply fly away. "Is life really so connected with the analysis which occupies our superficial consciousness?" asks Suzuki. He is far and beyond the spirit of the Greeks and of scholastic thinking; knowledge, as an ability to "position" ourselves or even as a way to approach God—as St. Thomas would have wanted it—is categorically discarded. Life, for Suzuki (and

---

²Erich Fromm, *To Have or to Be* (London: Abacus Books, 1976), p. 26.
³Daisetz Suzuki, *Zen and Japanese Culture* (Princeton: Princeton University Press, 1993), p. 264.
⁴Ibid., p. 250.

for the Japanese soul he is trying to describe) exists independent of "our intellectual deliberation and discrimination." Besides, he seems to imply ironically, there is always an uncertainty born from an everlasting residual of ignorance, which will defy anyhow our "scientific" calculations (whenever Suzuki uses the word *science* he puts it in quotation marks!). Facing this uncertainty, "Homo Sapiens is no better than the butterfly sleeping on the temple bell."[5] Thus, Daisetz Suzuki repeats in fact the conclusion of generations of Japanese thinkers, from the introduction of the Chang Zen, the Buddhism imported from China a thousand years before his days. Is there not in every one of us, he asks, a life very much deeper and larger than our intellectual deliberation and discrimination: the life of the Unconscious itself, of what he calls the "Cosmic Unconscious"?

Such a worldview cannot arrive at scientific reasoning simply because, voluntarily, it transcends it. This explanation seems to me more general and more appropriate than the first hypothesis—that of the love of nature—mentioned above. It holds true at least within the Buddhist-dominated traditions of India, China, and Japan. What should then fill our lives? "Our conscious life," maintains Suzuki, "gains its real significance only when it becomes connected with something more fundamental, namely, the Unconscious."[6] If the "Unconscious" is the "Transcendental," we find Suzuki in the company of the scholastic thinkers preceding by far the scientific revolution; or perhaps, very close to Husserl, who wanted to transcend it (see next chapter). The doubt about the "right way" in this world, as symbolized by the inverted dream of Chuang-tzu (who dreamt of himself as being a butterfly and when he woke up, asked himself whether a man dreamt of being a butterfly or the butterfly is dreaming that he is a man), is rejected by Suzuki, even though in his book he uses its symbolism to illustrate the role of "mutualism" and "becoming" in Zen. However, more important seems to me Suzuki's statement that, unlike the butterfly, we are in search of a "real significance." I found this to be one of the major inconsistencies in all the attempts to conceptualize Zen. Masao Abe put it in an elegant way: "Although Zen transcends human intellect, it does not exclude it." *Unconscious* sounds familiar, but this is not the Freudian "unconscious." It is "the true Self," that "emptiness" in which the Buddhahood is actualized.

How far are these ideas from Western ways of thinking, from Aristotle, from Thomism, from any pre-GN or post-GN thinking? When we read a sentence like *"That 'man's Mind'—the 'Mind' initially awakened*

---

[5]Ibid., p. 265.
[6]Ibid., p. 251.

in the Buddha himself as his own inner confirmation of himself as the authentic truth,"[7] we are reminded of Averroes and of the unity of the universal and the eternal Soul. A remark made by Suzuki also reminds one of medieval mystical thinking: "Faith is another word for the intuition of the Unconscious." This "faith" Suzuki is talking about may not be the faith of the Fathers of the Church, of Tertullian or Luther, but it has in common with them a mystical character eliminated from speculative thinking by Western science. How significant are these parallels to the questions posed at the beginning of the chapter? In Masao Abe's book, we find a very thorough, comparative discussion of the main metaphysical concepts of the East and West. Abe emphasizes that the concepts of *particular* and *universal*, *ji* and *ri* respectively, are extensively used in the Japanese versions of the Indian Mahayana Buddhism. Empiricism built upon the *ji* and idealism, built as in the Western tradition on the *ri*, which connotes the universal, the eternal, are in a permanent state of tension as modalities of knowledge. The East has found the solution to this contradiction in Nagarjuna's metaphysics based on the concept of *sunyata* or "Emptiness." "The opposition and tension between *ji* and *ri* which runs through human existence and ever makes human life problematic was for Nagarjuna to be resolved by Nothingness (*Mu*) which transcends the opposition between being and not-being, that is by 'Emptiness.'"[8] Abe realizes that such a sentence, even if it comes at the end of lengthy argumentations, is difficult for a Western mind. We cannot really understand Nothingness and Emptiness; since Parmenides, we know that only that which exists can be thought and what is thought, exists. The correspondence between subjective knowledge and the objective, external order has been, even if not always explicit, a constant of Western thought. It is very dangerous to make generalizations; my own presentation of the evolution within the Western way of thinking, from the Greeks to the dawn of the scientific revolution, states the reality of the change. Nothing really is constant in any tradition. Still, one cannot ignore certain patterns, certain things which *seem* to be true, constant, and almost self-evident: for instance, the fact that in India truth (*satya, dharma*) has an ethical character, very different from that of the West, that Being (*Atman*) is not something to be sought outside its seeker, because in the Indian tradition "being" cannot be separated from the subjective knower. *Satya* is, explains Maisson-Oursel in his well-known book on Indian civilization, the thing properly done, that which is as it should be, not some property

---

[7]Masao Abe, *Zen and Western Thought* (Honolulu: University of Hawaii Press, 1985), p. 105.
[8]Ibid., p. 94.

of an object. Truth meant for them being part of the natural order of the world, the *dharma*. When later, a new word synonymous to *satya* was introduced, *tathata*, it came to mean, in the Buddhist tradition, "suchness," as Masao Abe explains it. And even when the Japanese, in taking over these foreign concepts, modify them, the changes go in directions diverging from those of Western thought.

Nishida Kitaro, the founding father of the Kyoto school of philosophy, is a good illustration of this last point. In his works, he often pondered over these issues. In a conference delivered in 1919, in which he tried to position religious thought against the scientific one, he made clear a few of his ideas about science, scientific truth, and scientific reasoning.[9] Nishida defines clearly the way scientific "truth" is understood in the West, but then connects something we would call in Western parlance an "idealistic" point of view with Kantian epistemology. As a result, he concludes that "once an existent fits a certain 'category' we can *believe* it to exist." Since these a prioris thus formed are different from individual belief, truth thus acquired is objective. But this truth is ultimately based, one may contend, on something Nishida calls our *subjective/intuitive view* or a *pre-experiential self*. That is why objective scientific truth is still something internal to the human mind. Kantian, but not quite. There is another kind of knowledge built upon beliefs (defined as above), says Nishida, a "knowledge" based on even deeper structures, those of our affectivities/feelings. But this is superior knowledge (if one may use this word in this context), in the sense that this kind of "knowledge"—being based on affectivity—is the knowledge of the human soul, and "the soul in its entirety cannot be understood from the standpoint of knowledge." Why is this "knowledge of the soul" superior knowledge? Because knowledge is based on judgment, and judgment relies on the existence of subjects and predicates, and all the sentences about them are reunited in a whole, a whole in which these judgments take place. This "synthetical whole" is at the foundation of knowledge, therefore beyond it. Knowledge cannot know itself, says Nishida. (In a way this reminds us of some ideas of Husserl; but Nishida is different. In this work I cannot continue this analysis, but this subject is to be followed in another work on Shestov, Nishida, and Zen philosophy, in preparation.) For the purpose of our discussion, it is important just to close the circle and say that Nishida considers the truth based on affectivity as representing the essence of

---

[9]I thank here again Wayne Yokoyama, for making available a first draft of his translation of the talk "The Standpoint of Religion" delivered by Nishida in December 1919 at the Ryukoku University in Kyoto. This lecture is published in the *Complete Works* of Nishida Kitaro, in Japanese, v. 14, pp. 201-209.

Why Did the Far East Not Have Its Scientific Revolution? 67

religious thinking. It has often been claimed that Oriental thinkers did not develop sciences because they were deeply religious. This could be an example. But this kind of argument is a superficial one, to begin with, because the meaning of "being religious" can be, and certainly *is* in many instances, very differently understood by different cultures. It is clear, however, that both on metaphysical and practical grounds, Zen Buddhism could not find a privileged place for scientific reasoning.

It has also been often claimed that the Eastern societies did not develop a scientific thinking because they were dominated by irrational ways of thinking. (Again, we must be careful; a superficial rationalistic view could claim that irrational and religious ways of thinking are synonymous. While this may sometimes be true insofar as religious practice is concerned, it is certainly not true on purely theoretical grounds.) That also is a sweeping generalization, which does not withstand serious scrutiny. The great Indian and Chinese civilizations developed highly rational systems of thought. Max Weber, who made a clear distinction between knowledge in the East versus the West, pointed out that Confucianism (which is a significant part of the Chinese tradition, of course) was extremely rationalistic. His explanation for the absence of the scientific revolution in the East was based though on an idea which was only partly true: Weber claimed that the West achieved its scientific revolution because during the Renaissance and immediately after, it was ready to abandon all the restrictions imposed by tradition. The Orient was never able to free itself of tradition. First, as we have seen in the previous chapters, the evolution of Western thinking was a continuous process over time. There was no brutal separation from tradition; instead, the West changed through an accumulation of small (and granted, sometimes larger) changes and a constant adaptation of old intellectual tools to new tasks. But Max Weber is wrong on a factual basis too, at least insofar as India is concerned: the advent of Buddhism there represented just such a deep breach with the ancient Brahmanic-Vedantic tradition. In China, in spite of the very many different "ways" toward wisdom, there is indeed a "constant of thought" which has been embodied in Confucian thinking and is to be found to different extents—but always present—over China's entire intellectual history. Tradition in the Chinese way of thinking is represented by the postulate of the dialectical nature of the world. The contradiction between the opposites is at the origin of everything. The tension between *yin* and *yang* is at the same time a generating principle but also a dissolving one. From Heaven till man, everything could be represented as a manifestation of the two opposite principles. Too strong a presence of the opposites, perceived everywhere, can induce paralysis. I will lead to the utilitarianism of the Mohist philosophy, to the dissolving sophistry of Kung-sun Lung, and to the *wu wei* of Lao-tzu (who conceived Tao as *being* and *not being* at the same time). The truth is that the Chinese philosophy of this last millennium, called in the West Neo-Confucianism, was also dominated by this tradition. Another obstacle on the road to scientific reasoning may have been the inability of the Chinese to develop a formal logic. (The Indians had though more than one!) This may have had to do with their inability to discover the syllogism. This, in turn, is probably due to a certain imprecision in the structures of their language.[10] Leibnitz did not see in this a disadvantage; on the contrary, he was the first one in Europe to point out the advantages of a "pictographic" way of thinking. Chinese characters, through their ability to directly represent an object, gave him the idea to create a universal system of communication based on similar characters, which would represent at the same time the content of the message and the language though which the message would be conveyed. But it is not quite true to say that the ancient Chinese did not have a logical approach in their thinking. The Neo-Mohist school, in its fight against the Sophists, outlined a method of thinking, in *The Works of Mo-tzu*, based on a rigorous structuring of argumentations through definitions, proofs, etc. They classified the concepts into classes, general, generic, private, and found logical methods on which they could base their proofs. Moreover, they were close to breaking, on these grounds, the all-powerful tradition of the Chinese *contradictia oppoitorum* of the yin and yang, by arriving at the distinction between *universal* and *particular*.

The Judeo-Christian tradition has instilled deep in our minds a transcendental separated in an absolute way from ourselves. The dualistic attitude has become in the West a very deeply ingrained feature. Not only was God external to the thinking individual, but his fellowman, the objects he used, nature, everything was in front of him, opposite to him, facing him. At every moment, he had to cope with this duality. Western man ended by finding everything outside himself: his God as well as his truth, what he liked and what he disliked. As long as some of these things were still inside himself, as long as he had to look inward to find the most valuable things to him, he could not breakthrough. I propose to find the answer to the question posed in the title of this chapter in the following sentence: *Science was invented in the West because Western man succeeded in doing what his Eastern counterpart never wanted to do: he tore himself apart and firmly established the dualistic nature of "his" own world.* Not even in Confucian China was this the case. The Far East had insofar as the ability for abstract thinking goes

---

[10] A very good book on this subject is the classical work, in French, of Marcel Granet, *La Pensée chinoise* (Paris: Albin Michel, 1936).

everything the West had. There are many works to witness to that: see Stcherbatsky's and Needham's books, Oursel, Sivin and Granet on these subjects.[11] If anything, India had too much abstract thinking and China too much skepticism and practical utilitarianism. It is true that the political situation in these countries was very different from that in the West; also, their religions were different and their relationship to religious practice was different from those of the Westerners. Authors like Weber will tend to explain why the East did not undergo a scientific revolution in sociopolitical and theological terms. In all these explanations there is a grain (or more) of truth.

Not only did Eastern man refuse to accept the dualistic attitude of the West, but he preferred to turn away from the world and find the *locus* of his spiritual dwelling in himself. He rejoined the transcendental and merged into it. While it is easy to recognize in this attitude the Indian tradition, the Chinese were not foreign to it either. And this before and outside Buddhism; we can find in Lao-tzu and in Chuang-tzu many quotes to confirm this assertion. "Knowing the other is mere science; knowing thyself means true understanding," Chuang-tzu would say, and that says it all.

---

[11]See also Hajime Nakamura, *Ways of Thinking of Eastern Peoples* (Honolulu: Hawaii University Press, 1968) and references therein.

6
Disciplinarian Thinking

At the end of the first part of this work, I would like to focus upon the main idea I was trying to extract and distill in the previous chapter, that the scientific or the GN revolution, as I called it here, has created a new way of reasoning which is by its very nature "disciplinarian." I call it throughout this book *disciplinarian thinking*. This is a key point in a book about interdisciplinarity. The assumption that a disciplinarian thinking permeates *any* research activity in *all* the domains of research has two corollaries: one, that moving from discipline to discipline is not such a great adventure. In the process we use basically the same tools, we apply the same types of reasoning, briefly we submit ourselves to the one and the same *mathesis universalis*. "Interdisciplarity" is thus a limited enterprise, it is "weak" interdisciplinarity. It may sometimes be very successful and at other times very detrimental, as we shall see in the second part of the book. The second corollary is the ever recurrent attempt to make disciplines belonging to humanistic, social, economic, and political studies "scientific" by forcing upon them the above-mentioned "supermethod." From the early quarrels between natural philosophers and humanists (going back to the seventeenth century), to positivism in its various forms (from Comte to Reichenbach), to Dilthey who believed that modern philosophy (after Hegel) had lost its stature because it could not find a way to be "scientific," we witness the same story. Analytic philosophy and behaviorism were the last "heroic" attempts before the onset of the postmodernist movement which tries to solve the problem by overstepping it. Interdisciplinarity becomes the discipline of all the disciplines, that is, instead of being a mere technique it becomes the new "supramethod." As such, it has been renamed "transdisciplinarity." The second part of the book discusses these developments. In order to better frame this discussion, I want to clarify briefly in the following pages the nature of disciplinarian thinking.

One of the conclusions drawn from the preceding chapters is that in spite of the historical variety of this civilization we call "the Western world" or "Judeo-Christian civilization," there is a discernible continuity insofar as its patterns of thinking are concerned. Everything seems to begin in Greece, and Aristotle's shadow is ever present across the almost twenty centuries which bridge the gap between the beginning of philosophical thinking (which includes the first elements of "scientific" thinking) and the GN revolution. Even such a radical change as the introduction of Christianity in the vast pagan world dominated by Rome, and the instauration of Christian religious thinking in its realm, when translated into intellectual terms, becomes the history of the fusion between classical Greek philosophy and the new Christian theology. The Middle Ages, dominated at first by a problem originating in Plato (or more exactly in Neoplatonism), ended up by being strongly influenced by an Aristotelianism reshaped by Islamic and Jewish theologians. By the time the nominalists came out victorious in the quarrel over the "universals," the stage was set both for Francis Bacon and Descartes. We have sketched in the previous chapter a brief picture of the process in which, from a selective reading of Averroeian philosophy and a reaction to the Platonic Academy in Florence, a new skepticism was born in Padua. I hinted also at the role magic and "phantasmic thinking" played in creating certain epistemologic tools needed to develop the way of thinking leading to the GN revolution.

What has changed radically over these twenty centuries? For one thing, the fear and the repulsion that classical Greek philosophy (not the earlier, pre-Socratic one) had for certain concepts and ideas, such as infinity and movement, which introduced paradoxes and unsolvable contradictions in our reasoning. The ultimate goal of human thinking (as Aristotle pointed out in his *Metaphysics*) was *the knowledge of the first principles and causes*. Those were beyond Physics, the science of nature. Moreover, we have seen that the types of knowledge were organized in a hierarchic way. *Analytic thinking* and *demonstration* were practiced in mathematics and in "theoretical" thinking, but not in the lower kinds of reasoning and less worthy realms of existence. The "known" and the "unknown" were defined in a very peculiar way: whatever was worthy of consideration had an essence which had to be discovered. The object of knowledge had to be the relationship between *being* and its *essence*. In a way, the movement from "known" to "unknown" was muddled because of this confusion; certainly, any talk of a method to be developed to cover this gap between the known and the unknown was meaningless within this frame of thought. All this was to change during the sixteenth and the seventeenth centuries. The changes were announced by the thinkers of the fifteenth century; I mentioned Cusanus, Erasmus, and

Copernicus. And after them, Bruno, Bacon, Descartes, Galileo Galilei, and Newton. A careful reader who looks up dates may object that the notion of *mathesis universalis*—which I consider so important a factor in the birth of *disciplinarian thinking*—belongs to Leibnitz and Leibnitz was born in 1646. True, but the idea was in the air for more than a hundred years. It was first expressed as the *philosophia perennis* by Augustinus Eugubinus (born in 1497); the idea was that in all this seemingly disordered variety of philosophical beliefs and schools, there was something constant dominated by an inner logic which also was overseeing a permanent and steady growth of this body of knowledge. That implied method and purpose. Leibnitz, who was already surfing the crest of the GN revolution, was only giving expression, in his request for a systematization of the research in all sciences (or disciplines) along a common set of rules, to an already accepted sentiment that such rules exist.

Galileo Galilei himself has best expressed the change. In his *Libro della Natura* he wrote that philosophy (read knowledge as well as what can be known) is written in an endless book open in front of us at all times, that is, the surrounding universe. As simple as that: no first principles, no essences, no separation between lower and higher spheres. But, continues Galileo, one must understand the language in which the book is written. And the language, he concludes, is mathematics. The letters of the alphabet in which this language is written are geometric figures. That means that a method is needed in "reading," that demonstration is required to make the knowledge certain. We are far from Aristotle. A new relationship is thus established between the "known" and the "unknown": through an analytic method we must breakdown the problem to its components. The process continues till we understand the components; then, we can move from the "known" to the "unknown" guided by another method, a superior method or a "supermethod." That is the method which requires that every concept used in the description of the phenomenon and its parts be "mathematizable." Now this is not obvious. Mathematics is constraining; a "linear" relationship between two variables is very different from a "power" relationship. Moreover, mathematics imposes severe constraints through consistency requirements. One may "feel," "believe," or "think" that when we take a fast turn, we are acted upon by a force depending on the velocity at which we move, but within the confines of basic Galilean-Newtonian mechanics, this statement is not true. We must define "acceleration" as an operational concept to describe accurately the phenomenon. But, as I said already, this concept is not a direct one, a concept which can easily be obtained from the generalization of our immediate experiences. Later on, physics will introduce other new operational concepts, even further remote from immediate experience, such as those of "field" or "entropy," for instance. The very fact that new and counterintuitive concepts are needed to make the description of the phenomena coherent and consistent is also a revolutionary development in this new way of thinking. In a way, it seems like we are forcing nature to accept strange concepts (paradoxical, or even seemingly illogical) in order to extract knowledge. It is a violent approach, one which implies the idea of power. More exactly, it is not only the determination to "impose" our intellectual abilities in order to obtain knowledge but also the will to obtain power through knowledge. We remember Francis Bacon, of course, but also the general attitude of the Renaissance. This ability to accept concepts which are flexible, adaptable to the needs and the aims of our research, reminds us, of Giordano Bruno and his magical thinking as well. That is why I called this readiness to adapt our thinking to the constraints imposed by the mathematical rigors of the research "phantasmic thinking," and the corresponding concepts, "phantasmic concepts." It is a metaphor meant to remind us of the positive role played by certain long-abandoned and long-rejected ways of thinking, in molding our modern ways of thinking.

What makes a "discipline"? Obviously, its domain of interest is defined by that part or that aspect of the universe (including human beings) we choose to study. In that sense, there is a division between disciplines to be found in intellectual endeavors—in any civilization and at all times. The borders of the disciplines have changed often, but the mere existence of different areas of interest is an indisputable fact. What is important to our discussion, however, is a completely different point: what is really of interest in the context of a discussion about interdisciplinarity is to find the answer to the question *How is understanding and knowledge obtained within the borders of the discipline?* How do we distinguish between the flowers in a bouquet, regardless of their color? The great achievement of the GN revolution consisted in the creation of a *general methodology* and the establishment of a *unique purpose* for the intellectual activities we generically call today "research," *common to all disciplines*. This way of thinking is what I call *disciplinarian thinking*. It is based on very flexible concepts, which must respond to two basic requirements: they must be "adaptable" enough, in some cases, to the point that they can be far removed from the direct, sensory experience ("phantasmic") and they must be "mathematizable." *Disciplinarian thinking* incorporates the paradox: neither "paradoxical concepts," which lead to epistemological paradoxes (such as the concept of infinity), nor "paradoxical thinking," which is inducive of ontological paradoxes (such as those encountered in quantum mechanics or in modern "string theory" in physics), are illegitimate. It is essentially reductionist, even in its recent efforts to challenge complexity by means of novel concepts such as *information content, emergence,* or *deterministic chaos* and through theories based on such concepts. *Disciplinarian thinking* is purpose-oriented, teleological. It is driven by an idea which, until very recent times, was a self-fulfilling prophecy: the more we know, the better (off) we are. Today the "drive-for-power" element is more conspicuous, and technology, the offspring of parts of this disciplinarian thinking, tends to shift the discussion somewhat (see Heidegger's essay "The Question Concerning Technology" and the discussions raised by and around his ideas in this direction).

"Phantasmic concepts" and their "coupling" with mathematics is a very interesting issue in the context of our subject. I do not refer here to the attempts to formalize a discourse, like the *more geometrico* applied by Spinoza to present his "theory" of Ethics. This kind of adoption of mathematics to formalize philosophy has a tradition in modern times, from Kant (in his *Critique of Pure Reason*) to Bertrand Russell. Conversely, formalized logic has been used to analyze philosophical texts (like in the case of Carnap's "deconstruction" of certain parts of Heidegger's *Being and Time*). In a section of *What Is a Thing?* entitled "The Mathematical, Mathesis," Heidegger discusses the nature of the "mathematical" in the Greek context and in that of his own theory of knowledge. It is not our purpose to follow this discussion here; I shall only borrow some of his definitions and bring forth one idea which I find important for our topic: "Mathesis means learning; mathemata what is learnable," writes Heidegger.[1] He tries to understand to what learning through mathematics applies by comparing the concept to other concepts such as *physica, poioumena, chremata, pragmata,* etc. Each defines classes of objects revealed through the study of the domain described by each of the above concepts (words). To which class does "mathemata" apply? To numbers? If so, argues Heidegger, it is not because the mathematical is numerical in character, but because the numerical is something mathematical. Why does he make this choice? I suppose that many will say that his choice goes in this direction, because that is how Heidegger confirms his theory of knowledge as the "unfolding" of the already known. I think however that he may have been set on this track by a familiarity with David Hilbert's work on the "axiomatization" of Euclidean geometry. In his *Fundaments of Geometry* (*Grundlagen der Geometrie*), published in 1899, Hilbert shows that by choosing five groups of axioms and applying them to three categories of abstract objects, we can combine them through logical operations and thus obtain an entirely consistent set of relations between these objects. Now, if we interpret these abstract objects as

---

[1] Martin Heidegger, *Basic Writings* (New York: Harper and Row, 1977), p. 251.

points, straight lines, and planes respectively, the "set of relations" mentioned above becomes the rules and the theorems of Euclidean geometry! This would constitute a proof that the "quantitative" is not necessarily an attribute of the mathematical construct. Beyond mathematical theories we find therefore logical structures, not necessarily related to anything quantitative.

"The *mathemata*, the mathematical, is that 'about' the things we already know," writes Heidegger, and adds: "Therefore, we do not first get it out of things, but, in a certain way, we bring it already with us."[2] Thus numbers become "mathematical" simply because they are often used in dealing with things, in bringing forth a first, direct knowledge of things. This conclusion is in agreement with the seemingly nonquantitative (or, not necessarily nonquantitative) character of mathematics, inferred from Hilbert (and others who followed him in this direction). That would imply then, that mathematical theories can indeed be applied to any field of research; Bergson's criticism and his claim that mathematical description—being limited to the quantitative—cannot describe phenomena related to life and living beings, which are characterized by the "qualitative," turn out to be mistaken. Yes and no, would be my comment. The structure of mathematical theory is dominated by a logic which is "overseeing" it. Once the kind of logic used is established (one can erect structures built on multivalued logics too), one has to stay with it, consistently, otherwise the theory will lose its consistency. The trouble is that in complex systems, such as living organisms or social systems, the description of the system may require the simultaneous application of several types of mathematical constructs; connecting the various "logics" underlying these constructs is not a trivial matter. It may even be impossible, in a dynamical situation, that is, if these "couplings" of logical understructures change in time. In such cases it would seem that a "mathematical treatment" would lead nowhere, but not necessarily because of the impossibility of quantifying the constitutive concepts of that given discipline.

I would stop one more time at Heidegger's text: "As axiomatic, the mathematical project is the anticipation of the essence of things."[3] If the mathematical project is one of the "unfolding of the truth," if we seek structures we know to exist, we can perform these intellectual acts only if equipped with the appropriate concepts. One could argue that on the contrary, based upon what has been said above, it is the structure of the mathematical theory which is determinant and not its specific objects. But not any kinds of objects can be fitted into a given theory; the

---

[2]Ibid., p. 252.
[3]Ibid., p. 268.

"phantasmic concept" of the metric tensor, used by Einstein in general relativity to describe the geometry of a curved space-time, would not fit into Euclidean geometry. That is why I said previously that a relationship must exist between the phantasmic concepts, the mathematical structure required to support them, and the teleological principle which guides the research. This pattern is at work in all modern disciplines. Again, this is *disciplinarian thinking*.

I think that Husserl was acutely aware of the difficulty in practicing disciplinarian thinking in the realm of the humanities and the social sciences. He mentioned Dilthey's (and others', like Rickett's and Windelband's) efforts to apply this way of thinking to philosophy; unlike them however, Husserl believed that a deep change must take place in our ways of handling the object(s) of the human (humanistic) studies. In his long essay "Philosophy and the Crisis of the European Man," Husserl discusses the relationship between the scientific approach to nature, or in his words "the mathematical science of nature," and "the explanation of the spiritual."[4] In the incompatibility between the two, he sees the core of the contemporary European crisis. The content of this essay is relevant for the discussion concerning disciplinarian thinking, as well as for the discussion, taken up in the next chapters of this book, of the conflict between the "two cultures" and the meaning of the interdisciplinarian endeavor. Here, we shall refer only to the first aspect. Husserl recognizes the tremendous success of natural science: "Mathematical science of nature is a technical marvel for the purpose of accomplishing inductions whose fruitfulness, probability, exactitude and calculability, could previously not even be suspected. As an accomplishment it is a triumph of the human spirit."[5] The problem arises when this successful science is extended to the knowledge of the spirit. The spirit is objectified, it becomes "real" in the same sense nature is "real," and thus it is "explained" on the same grounds as the physical. But, contends Husserl, "To speak of the spirit as reality (Realität), presumably a real (reallen) annex to bodies and having its supposedly spatiotemporal being within nature, is an absurdity."[6] This is the heart of the matter; how then should one treat the subjective, the "spirit"? First, we must rid ourselves of the naive idea of "objectivism," this idea which makes nature and spirit realities of the same kind. Next we must understand that the sciences of

---

[4]Edmund Husserl, *Phenomenology and the Crisis of Philosophy* (New York: Harper and Row, 1965). The essay under discussion is a revised version of a lecture delivered by Husserl in Vienna in 1935. It is a late work, reflecting the phenomenological philosophy of the author developed to its most advanced stage.
[5]Ibid., p. 186.
[6]Ibid., p. 185.

nature are not truly rational and objective since they presuppose as data "principles that are themselves thoroughly lacking in actual rationality," or in other words, the facts are already intended as truths. (Is that what Heidegger meant when he wrote in the above-mentioned essay, "Upon the basis of the mathematical, the *experientia* becomes the modern experiment"?)[7] Therefore, "the ego that acts and is acted upon," which is not part of nature or parallel to it, but another isolated thing in the world among others, has to be treated in a fundamentally different way. That way is that of Husserl's *transcendental phenomenology*. It is, claims its author, the only way to overcome the "naturalistic objectivism" of scientific reasoning, which is nothing else but disciplinarian thinking. "The development of a real method of grasping the fundamental essence of spirit in its intentionalities and consequently of instituting an analysis of spirit with a consistency reaching to the infinite, led to transcendental phenomenology. It was this that overcame naturalistic objectivism, and for that matter, any form of objectivism, in the only possible way, *by beginning one's philosophizing from one's ego*."[8] Here Husserl hints at a "new scientific thinking," in which the *ratio* is the spirit understanding itself and in which "nature fits as a product of the spirit." This would be different from disciplinarian thinking, but what is it, really?

I would close this brief "theoretical discussion" of the content of the first part of the book by remarking that in view of all the above, it is not surprising to find so many instances of "interferences" between disciplines. Interdisciplinarity should not be a rare occurrence. After Husserl and Heidegger though, the so-called imperialistic tendencies of "scientism" have been often decried. That is, the tendency of "hard" sciences (most of the time, physics) to mix into the "internal affairs" of such fields as sociology, history, or even literature have been harshly criticized. There seems to be a deepening contradiction at work, both in the domain of the methodology and in that of the interaction between various groups involved in research and intellectual activities. To these matters the second part of this book is dedicated.

---

[7]Heidegger, p. 269.
[8]Husserl, p. 190.

7

Interdisciplinarity, Old and New

I do not consider the mere use of mathematics *in any discipline* an interdisciplinarian activity. After having read the first part of this book, it must be apparent why. As we have seen, *disciplinarian thinking* represents the intellectual (epistemological) basis for any discipline (*scientia*). It is a way of thinking characterized by the exclusive use of concepts adapted and/or adaptable to some form of mathematization and submitted to its underlying logic. There are disciplines in which these desiderata are fulfilled; there are others, in which it is very difficult to achieve these requirements. In the first case, the extensive use of mathematics and quantitative analysis within these disciplines is justified and successful. In the second case, the compulsive effort toward rigorousness through the "mathematization" of a discipline (such as political science or Freudian psychology) becomes merely *quantofrenia*, as someone has sarcastically labeled the hopeless effort. Of course, a "decent" use of statistics in the social sciences, for instance, is perfectly legitimate, and there are domains of sociology and anthropology which have successfully incorporated mathematical techniques. The question we shall ask here is to what extent is the use of concepts, intellectual constructs, or even laws (such as "conservation laws"), when transferred from one discipline to another, "interdisciplinarian." In order to even attempt an answer to this question, we first had to come, in the previous chapters, to a clear understanding of the nature of disciplinarian research, which in turn led us to a definition—even if somewhat fragile—of "interdisciplinarity." Of course, the trivial approach would be simply to state that the intelligent use of a concept taken from one field (or discipline)—physics, for example—and its application to another one—for instance, economics—represents an interdisciplinarian approach. Thus, a book entitled *The Entropy Law and the Economic Process* sounds like the summary of an interdisciplinarian enterprise. But even at this level of analysis, we are faced with a nontrivial question concerning the nature of the interdisciplinarian activity: Is this physics applied to economics, or is it a new kind of economics? I hinted already at the "disciplinarian divide," and we shall have in the next two chapters a brief but hopefully edifying glance at the difficulties arising from the interferences between cultures as well as between disciplines. There are many questions involved concerning the nature of the "tools" used in various disciplines and the ways these "tools" are "shifted" (or even changed) when moved from one domain to another (do we use metaphors, do we transfer operational concepts?). These are also implicit questions about the boundaries of the disciplines, and as a result they bear on our discussion of interdisciplinarity. The word *interdisciplinarity* itself had its times of glory: as an independent and explicit concept, it has been defined in a sociological context. "Interdisciplinarity was probably born in New York City in the mid 1920s, most likely at the corner of 42nd and Madison. The word seems to have begun life in the corridors of the Social Science Research Council as a kind of bureaucratic shorthand for what the council saw as its chief function, the promotion of research that involved two or more of its seven constituent societies....By mid-century interdisciplinarity was common coin in the social sciences...by the late 50s, the idea even seemed old-hat."[1] What is the difference between interdisciplinarity, transdisciplinarity, multidisciplinarity, intradisciplinarity, metadisciplinarity?[2] We shall soon discuss these concepts, but first let us consider for a moment a down-to-earth, "first-approximation" interpretation of the term *interdisciplinarity*. The key is in the word *intelligent*. How should I know, while working inside a discipline, whether I am using a "foreign," an "imported," concept intelligently, that is, in a way which is compatible with its original meaning but also with its new context? For instance, if *entropy* describes the degree of randomness (or departure from order) in a physical system at a given moment in its evolution, and I try to find a measure of order (or disorder) within, say, a given social group, under which constraints can I use this concept in the interpretation of a piece of anthropological fieldwork? The human beings I study are not the hypothetical molecules of an ideal gas; their interactions are governed by laws which are radically different. Suppose however that I do it "right." Would the

---

[1] Quoted from "Interdisciplinarity: The First Half Century," an article by Roberta Franck published in E.G. Stanley and T.F. Hoad, eds., *Words: For Robert Burchfield's Sixty-Fifth Birthday* (Cambridge: D.S. Brewer, 1988), pp. 91, 96.
[2] A discussion of these concepts may be found in Julie Thompson Klein, *Crossing Boundaries: Knowledge, Disciplinarities, and Interdisciplinarities* (Charlottesville and London: University Press of Virginia, 1996), in particular chap. 2.

definition of interdisciplinarity be then, simply, "the correct use of concepts belonging to one discipline in another"?

Let us consider an example: in chemistry, the concept of "potential energy" has been adopted as an extension of the same idea in physics. However, the "potential" as used by chemists to describe the binding energy of molecules has been transformed to the point that physics students who take an introductory course in physical chemistry have, at first, difficulty in understanding it. The "correct use" is in fact a new use. Indeed, talking about the "potential energy" of an atom, in the same sense as that used for a stone above our head or an aircraft in flight, has no meaning; in physics, at first, potential energy was related to the law of gravitational attraction. Thus "potential" and "mass" are related. But at the atomic level, the electrical forces become many orders of magnitude more intense than the gravitational ones; for that reason, the attraction or the repulsion at very small distances, described by a "potential curve," becomes the appropriate concept to describe the interaction. A molecule is formed when the two forces (of attraction and repulsion) are equilibrated, and as a result, a stable situation is reached: the two (or more) atoms will stick together until some external force upsets this state of equilibrium. One can compare this situation with that of a tiny ball sitting at the lowest point of a concave surface. That is why the chemist will describe the molecule in its stable state as lying in a "potential well." Next, let us consider a somewhat related but a much more complicated example: In the introduction I mentioned Erwin Schrödinger's contribution to biology and life sciences, as presented in the texts included in his booklet entitled *What is Life?* In a series of lectures delivered during the war (1943) at Trinity College in Dublin, Scrödinger set out to look at "the physical aspects of the living cell." These were the reflections of a physicist around the question: "How can the events in space and time which take place between the spatial boundary of a living organism be accounted for by physics and chemistry?"[3] In fact, Schrödinger was puzzled by the observation that genes, which were recently discovered to be the carriers of hereditary mechanisms, were extremely small. They barely occupied, according to the experimental estimates made by C.D. Darlington, a cubic volume having a 300A edge. That meant no more than roughly one million atoms in the volume, "a number much too small to entail an orderly and lawful behavior according to statistical physics, and *that means according to physics*."[4] Schrödinger the physicist had analyzed a problem in biology using

---

[3]Erwin Schrödinger, *What Is Life?* (Cambridge: Cambridge University Press, 1996), p. 3.
[4]Ibid., p. 30; my emphasis.

concepts and laws belonging to his discipline, physics. We may call this procedure "interdisciplinarian." But let us follow his reasoning: the fact that genes carry a function which is rigorously reproducible seems to contradict the postulates of the physics governing the atoms composing it: "How can we from the point of view of the statistical physics reconcile the facts that the gene structure seems to involve only a comparatively small number of atoms...and that nevertheless it displays a most regular and lawful activity—with a durability or permanence that borders upon the miraculous?"[5] Fluctuations in the positions of the atoms which compose the tiny gene would prevent the transmission of any fixed properties. The assumption is, of course, that a fixed structure is associated with the functional properties. This fixed structure cannot be conserved unless it is a well-defined molecular structure and not simply a collection of atoms. The molecule is characterized by a certain stability, due to the "potential well" in which the entire structure lies. For this stability to be upset at a given ambient temperature (which is equivalent to saying, at a given energy level), a significant amount of energy has to be imparted to the atomic structure which has organized itself in a molecular state. If this energy is not furnished by a source external to the system, the probability that a change will occur at a temperature comparable to the potential at which the molecule is stable (i.e., lies within the potential well), is small. In other words, the time scale for such a change to occur will be very long. This is Schrödinger's argumentation and he concludes: "We may safely assert that there is no alternative to the molecular explanation of the hereditary substance."[6] In the next step of his analysis, he points out that the molecule must have in common with the crystal (solid) a fixed structure, or as he puts it, a small molecule might be called "the germ of a solid." Then comes Schrödinger's mental "jump": from such solid germs, a crystal can be built by simply repeating the same structure in three dimensions. However, unlike in the case of the natural crystal, here an extended structure is formed, an aggregate in which every atom, every group of atoms, plays an individual role, *"not entirely equivalent with that fo many others."*[7] This crystal is not however a regular crystal but one with an *aperiodic structure*. This idea of the "aperiodic crystal" is the core of Schrödinger's contribution to biological sciences: "We believe," he wrote, "a gene—or perhaps the whole chromosome fiber—to be an aperiodic solid."[8] Fifty years later in the introduction to their commemorative book dedicated to Schrödinger's

---

[5] Ibid., p. 46.
[6] Ibid., p. 57.
[7] Ibid., p. 60; my emphasis.
[8] Ibid., p. 61.

contributions to biology, Michael Murphy and Luke O'Neill summarized thus his interdisciplinarian contribution: "The problem faced by the cell was how a gene...could survive thermal disruption and still pass on information to future generations. Schrödinger proposed that to avoid this problem the gene was most probably some kind of aperiodic crystal which stored information as a codescript in its structure...this prophetic statement has been shown to be true by work on the structure of DNA which lead to the central dogma of molecular biology."[9]

How did Schrödinger proceed in his interdisciplinary endeavor? He did not change in any way his ways of reasoning, which were those of a physicist. He was truly and entirely "disciplinarian" in his thinking; the key concepts of *his* discipline were used "correctly," that is, within the confines of the specific laws of the discipline. A *physicist* comes to the conclusion that an operational concept basic in *chemistry*—the molecule—has to be used in a somewhat modified way in *biology*. He takes the concept and modifies it—to that of the aperiodic crystal or (macro)molecule—so that it becomes appropriate to the new discipline (biology) in which is to be used. The physical-chemical concepts are not used as "metaphors" and the analysis through which the concepts are transformed takes into account both the elements specific to the domains of physics/chemistry and biology. I consider this to be an example of *positive interdisciplinarity* entirely within the frame of disciplinarian thinking. While retaining the basic postulates of disciplinarity and in agreement with its unifying postulates, with its *mathesis universalis*, positive interdisciplinarity *transforms* the concepts belonging to a given discipline and *recreates* them, so that they become operational within a new discipline. Whenever this path is followed, the interdisciplinarian approach is successful in the sense that it may lead to a major contribution in a given domain of research; as a result disciplines may be changed in very significant ways, without being voided of their content or deprived of their right to continue to exist as a result of the impact of such a *positive interdisciplinarity*. Biology did not become biochemistry or biophysics, but it incorporated them.

Let us return now and consider the various terms used to describe interactions between disciplines that we mentioned before. One of the most interesting works I read on the subject, as I was preparing my lectures on "interdisciplinarity," was a book entitled *Conceptual Foundations for Multidisciplinary Thinking*. The author, Stephen J. Kline, was involved for some twenty years in a very interesting interdisciplinary program at Stanford University. He points out from the

---

[9]Michael P. Murphy and Luke A.J. O'Neill, eds., *What Is Life? The Next Fifty Years*, (Cambridge: Cambridge University Press, 1995), p. 2.

very beginning that "multidisciplinary discourse is not what we usually mean by interdisciplinary study."[10] What is therefore "multidisciplinarian discourse?" It is, according to Kline, the totality of the discussion concerning the ways truth assertions are achieved in various disciplines, the ways in which they can or should be compared, but also the questions concerning the validity of such comparisons. In addition, it applies to questions such as "Is the reductionist approach, characteristic of 'hard' sciences, appropriate and/or sufficient when applied in other domains?" The book sets off to cover a long list of topics, among them: "the delineation of what a given discipline can (and cannot) represent in the world...the development of insight into the similarities and differences of the disciplines...how the disciplines ought to constrain each other when applied to problems that inherently require knowledge from many disciplines, etc."[11] Even though no claim is made concerning the importance of these topics, Kline assumes that the development of a multidisciplinary discourse will help do several things: First, it will help alleviate a pervasive anxiety permeating our time which has its origin in the "inability to perceive the human knowledge as a whole." But as if scared of such a broad scope, the author hastens to add that multidisciplinary discourse will neither solve the problem of this "universal anxiety," nor is it meant to replace disciplinary work. It will rather "help disciplinary experts better understand the connection of their own field to the whole of the human knowledge."[12] There are also pragmatic reasons, which are obvious enough, therefore I will skip them. I would like to mention however another argument in favor of multidisciplinarian discourse, an argument discussed at some length in Kline's book, which I also find very important. (Since I decided not to discuss "complexity" in the present book, I shall only mention this topic here, and point out its importance; its detailed discussion will be the subject of another work.) The topic is that of "emergent properties." Complex systems, that is, systems containing subsystems which interact among themselves, are capable of exhibiting completely new properties, which, independently, none of the subsystems would posses. Multidisciplinarian discourse, writes Kline, will enable us to better understand "emergent properties." Indeed, in the process of developing this point, the author offers a very good quantitative analysis of complex systems. On the other hand, the conclusions reached by the author concerning the fundamental differences between the "principles" of the

---

[10]Stephen J. Kline, *Conceptual Foundations for Multidisciplinary Thinking* (Stanford: Stanford University Press, 1998), p. xiv.
[11]Ibid., p. 2.
[12]Ibid., p. 3.

Interdiscipinarity, Old and New

human sciences and those "that apply to inert, naturally-occurring objects," as the author defines the "hard" sciences, are most of the time interesting but not too surprising. Nor is the conclusion surprising that "neither the reductionist nor its opposing (synoptist) view is sufficient to treat all the problems of vital concern to humans."[13] After having defined carefully in the first part of the book the basic concepts to be used (systems, sysreps, and their relationship with the human mind; see the first three chapters), Kline discusses in the second and third part of the book the key issues of "complexity" and "structure." Only by the fourteenth chapter are we supposed to have learned enough on the subject to be able to consider a few examples of "multidisciplinary analysis." I will very briefly present only one such example. It has to do with "sociotechnical systems" and Ernst Cassirer, the contemporary Neo-Kantian philosopher. The above systems (i.e., sociotechnical systems) are "systems that link people with human made hardware to perform tasks that humans want done."[14] Such systems have a long history (which goes back to times that precede Homo sapiens apparently); the author presents a figure which shows various "curves of growth of human powers" (for instance, memory storage capacity, precision in machining, speed of communication, etc.) over the years. The figure indicates that all the (ten) curves presented are doubly exponential in time and most of the rise occurs after 1840. The analysis of the human sociotechnical system in the context of complexity and human designed feedbacks leads Kline to the conclusion that "the use of innovation and perpetuation of innovations in the sociotechnical systems through culture distinguishes us from other animals in a qualitative way."[15] The accent is on the qualitative. Here Cassirer enters: In his book *An Essay on Man*, Cassirer claims that humans are not distinguished from animals in a qualitative way, but only in a quantitative one. Any essential difference between humans and developed animals, such as the use of "symbolic forms" or the ability to set ourselves long-term goals, are mere quantitative differences. For instance, Cassirer claims, our "symbolic forms" are only of a far greater complexity than the animal ones, but not really different, etc. Why did the philosopher reach the wrong conclusion? asks Kline. He was quite thorough in his enterprise: he studied human art, science, myth, religion, language, and history. But he studied them separately: "Cassirer did not consider sociotechnical systems or other systems that combine many human activities." And the conclusion is: "What we see, then, is the following: long studies of

---

[13]Ibid., p. xiv.
[14]Ibid, p. 171.
[15]Ibid., p. 176.

individual disciplines and literatures by many able scholars did not reveal a qualitative difference between humans and other animals. Study of sociotechnical systems does, rather quickly."[16]

Transdisciplinarity is the title of a book by Basarab Nicolescu, recently published in France. (To my knowledge it has not yet been translated into English; all the quotes in the following are my translations from the French original.) The main thrust of this book is different from both the present one and that of Kline. The title of one of the chapters of the book, "Transdisciplinarity—A New Worldview," gives the reader a direction, at the first glance. A direct confrontation of the ideas presented here with those of Nicolescu's book would not therefore be too useful. ("Complexity" turns out to be a very important concept in the author's quest for a new worldview, and this opens an avenue for a discussion in the future.) However, I will try to explain the meaning of "transdisciplinarity" for Nicolescu. First, let us see what is not *transdisciplinarity* in his view. As the reader may have guessed by now, *interdisciplinarity* is not synonymous with *transdisciplinarity*. Interdisciplinarity is a mere transfer of methods from one discipline into another. There are three degrees of interdisciplinarity, writes Nicolescu: one is that of the "transfer," such as when methods of nuclear physics transferred to medicine offer a new way to cure cancer. The second is the "epistemological" degree, which represents a transfer of a "tool," such as that of formal logic, to the domain of law studies. As a result, interesting and new conclusions are obtained in the area of the epistemology of the law. Finally, there is a third degree of interdisciplinarity, through which new disciplines can be created: for instance, the transfer to astrophysics of the ideas and methods pertaining to particle physics led to the creation of the new field of quantum cosmology. There is also *multidisciplinarity*, adds Nicolescu, and it is interesting to compare his view with Kline's. "*Multidisciplinarity represents the study of a subject belonging to one given discipline, by means belonging to several other disciplines.*"[17] As an example, the author gives the study of a painting by Giotto in which the point of view of the history of art is confronted with others based in physics, chemistry, history of religions, European history, and geometry. The object under study is thus better understood, but the study remains confined to its discipline. We have just seen however that Cassirer, while studying the human being, did just that, and seemingly came to the wrong conclusion. Multidisciplinarity is defined by Nicolescu in a simpler (and perhaps a somewhat more simplistic) way than that of Kline. The communication between the disciplines brought together in

---

[16]Ibid., p. 177.
[17]Basarab Nicolescu, *La Transdisciplinarité* (Paris: Editions du Rocher, 1996), p. 64.

Interdisciplinarity, Old and New 87

the multidisciplinarian enterprise is neglected by Nicolescu, who aims at transdisciplinarity mainly. In any event, his conclusion is that both inter- and multidisciplinarity are ultimately relevant only inside a given discipline. (In our terms, both would represent "weak," or at best "positive," interdisciplinarity.) On the other hand, in opposition with these two, transdisciplinarity must address that which is at the same time *between* the disciplines, *across* the disciplines (*à travers les différentes disciplines*, in the French text) and *beyond* the disciplines. "Its purpose (that is, of transdisciplinarity) must be *the understanding of the present world*, which requires a unity of knowledge."[18] It is obvious, even after such a succinct and crude presentation of the terms, that in Nicolescu's view transdisciplinarity is a new way of knowing, a new epistemology which in turn requires a new ontology. The new reality we thus discover will be structured on several "levels of reality," in the author's terminology. The disciplinarian research (not to be confounded with the disciplinarian thinking as I defined it in this book) is confined only to one level of reality. Worse even, it only addresses fragments of that one and partial reality. Transdisciplinarity, on the contrary, is meant to address the "dynamics triggered by the simultaneous manifestation of several levels of reality."[19] Therefore the scope of transdisciplinarity, as defined by Basarab Nicolescu, vastly transcends our more limited interest while discussing disciplines and interdisciplinarity. One can see, however, that dealing with interdisciplinarian subjects can become a discipline in itself, but also in a given context, a new discipline which transcends the traditional disciplines; it may become the a new epistemological tool. The word *metadiscipline* in the title of my book hint at these two (very) different possible interpretations of interdisciplinarity.

In this book, we discuss a few examples of what one might call "botched" interdisciplinarity. The French psychiatrist Jacques Lacan (as we shall see in more detail in the next chapters) seems to have been one of its champions, with his confused and confusing use of concepts imported from mathematics into psychology. In the book by Sokal and Bricmont (see chapter 9) there were many other names mentioned in the context of "muddled thinking." (In order to avoid a polemical tone, I will abstain from talking of "intellectual impostors.") It would be easy, in fact, to find an endless number of examples of the nonsensical use of imported concepts, or of the incorrect application of laws transferred from one domain to the other. However, the aim of this work is not to take issue with the representatives of the so-called cultural constructivism, an intellectual trend based on what has been ironically

---

[18]Ibid., p. 66.
[19]Ibid., p. 67.

labeled "do-it-yourself epistemologies." Neither do I intend to add my voice to that of my colleagues who embarked on a crusade against the "muddleheadedness." As a result of these recent developments, we witness a reversal of the situation pictured by C.P. Snow: it seems that nowadays it is not anymore triumphant science which, marching aggressively toward glorious achievements, brutally pushes aside helpless literary intellectuals. On the contrary, today science seems nervous and insecure and if aggressive, it is so because not being understood it has become the victim of arbitrary judgment and, worse even, a victim of unjust condemnation. This new situation develops in a new realm created by a combination of constructivist historians, a new brand of sociologists of science, and feminist epistemologists. It is a dramatic and real fight, very well documented by two scientists, Gross and Levitt, in their relatively recent book *Higher Superstition*. I believe that this is a very important issue; in this book however, I will try to go beyond it, and present the interaction between disciplines in a more specific and at the same time in a more general way. My analysis will be guided by the idea developed here that since disciplinarian thinking is at the root of both modern and postmodern ways of thinking, on a deeper level the conflict is elsewhere. I do not ask here what motivates Lacan or Fox Keller, Baudrillard or Heyles, I simply look at their interdisciplinary discourse and conclude that as it is, it cannot contribute in any positive way to science. Worse even, their discourse (narrative?) does not create really a new discipline (that possible, perhaps, metadiscipline I alluded to above) out of which a radically new approach to research could develop. Their disciplinarian thinking limits the efficiency of their analysis to abstract, "stripped-down" entities ultimately irrelevant in humanistic studies. When described in the realm of disciplinarian thinking, human beings are stripped of their individuality; that is necessary in order to be able to associate their behavior with the "phantasmic concepts" we build for the purpose of constructing the so-called humanistic sciences. The tremendous failures of this century's social-engineering experiments, on the left as well as on the right, show how impossible this task is. In his counterattack against the C.P. Snow text (discussed in more detail in the next chapter), F.R. Leavis made an argument in this direction, illustrated by a quoted taken from a novel written by D.H. Lawrence: "We are all abstractly and mathematically equal, if you like. Every man has hunger and thirst, two eyes, one nose and two legs. We're all the same in point of number. But spiritually, there is a pure difference and neither equality nor inequality counts."[20]

---

[20]Frank R. Leavis, *Two Cultures? The Significance of C.P. Snow* (New York: Pantheon Books, 1963), p. 40.

There is also an "illusory" interdisciplinarity, born through a process to some extent similar to that of "positive interdisciplinarity." In this case however, in the process of transfering the concepts or the laws from one discipline to the other, something goes wrong. A good example is the birth of the neoclassical economic theory from the adaptation of the Hamilton-Jacobi formalism developed in theoretical mechanics; this case has been extensively discussed by Philip Mirowski in his book *More Heat than Light*. In a nutshell, the author presents the problem the following way: "The progenitors of neoclassical economic theory boldly copied the reigning physical theories in the 1870s. The further one digs, the greater the realization that those neoclassicals did not imitate physics in a desultory or superficial manner; no, they copied their models mostly term for term and symbol for symbol and said so."[21] After that, the author continues and in over four hundred pages shows how neoclassical economics from Jevons and Walras till Samuelson and beyond had failed because it wrongly used a metaphor borrowed elsewhere (physics). To make things worse economists also used the wrong way analogies and homologies with the natural sciences.[22] Moreover, while physics has moved away from the "metaphor" of energy, replacing heat with light as the central concept or metaphor for their science, economists, claims Mirowski, stuck to their mechanistic worldview. The explanation of why this happened is implied to some degree but it is not obvious; however, the detailed analysis of the transfer of "tools" and techniques from one discipline to the other is very instructive and relevant for any discussion about the meaning and the limits of interdisciplinarity.

This brief presentation of successful, partially successful, as well as downright botched cases of interdisciplinarity raises the question of whether one should concentrate on the sociohistoric causes of the failure (or success), or rather on the "technical" ones. Were the economists under the spell of the metaphor of the conservation of energy because we all, regardless of the discipline to which we belong, are for some reason, torn between the acceptance and/or rejection of certain archetypal concepts such as identity and diversity, invariance and change? (We remember here, together with Mirowski, the French philosopher of science, Emile Meyerson.) But then why did the physicists not fall into the same trap? It might be argued that the economists could not realize

---

[21]Philip Mirowski, *More Heat than Light* (Cambridge: Cambridge University Press, 1989), p. 3.
[22]That point is very well discussed in an article by I. Bernard Cohen, in a collective volume dedicated to a critical appraisal of Mirowski's book, *Non-Natural Social Science: Reflecting on the Entreprise of "More Heat than Light"* Durham and London: Duke University Press, 1993).

their error soon enough because of the lack of a stable field of research such as that offered by nature to the researchers in physics (or other "hard" sciences). While searching for operational concepts, the economist has to take into account historical, political, anthropological, and many other factors. To find out if "utility" or "value" is conserved in a given society, at a given moment in its (economic) history, is much more difficult than to decide about conservation of "energy" or "momentum" in a collision between two perfectly elastic balls. However, when a certain mathematical formalism is applied, the problem becomes more restricted: regardless of whether analogy, homology, or metaphor is used, one must know under what condition a certain formalism can be applied. In another book, *Against Mechanism*, Mirowski presents a very good illustration of the "blindness" of one of the founding fathers of neoclassical economics, Walras, to the warnings of a French mathematician (Laurent) concerning the basic definition and the meaning of terms supposed to be used in Hamiltonian formalism. He mentions also the exchange between Gibbs, probably the most famous American physicist of his time, and Irving Fisher, the author of *Mathematical Investigations in the Theory of Value and Prices*.[23]

We could single out therefore cases of *successful, illusory,* and *botched* interdisciplinarity. The classification is based on a value judgment of the end result of the interdisciplinarian endeavor. While it is clear that the first case, exemplified through the activity of Schrödinger (there were more famous physicists who joined biological sciences at around the same time, for instance, Delbrück or Leo Szilard), can be defined as a "success," one may argue that there are positive realizations within neoclassical economics as well (see the large number of Nobel laureates in economics; ultimately, the proof is in the pudding, isn't it?). And concerning the "botched interdisciplinarity" is concerned, I imagine that there will be a number of authors who will be upset by my statement and reject it with anger. "You talk from a subjective, restricted, narrow point of view," they will say. "That is the point of view of the physicist, the point of view of scientism." "No, not at all," I will reply. My point is in fact simple: the vast majority of postmodernist arguments are made from the standpoint of the same *disciplinarian thinking*. As I wrote above, once having stated this, I have a criterion to judge interdisciplinarian practice.

To conclude this chapter, I would like to return to an issue mentioned at its very beginning: the use of mathematics in disciplines which are hardly quantifiable. If the use of mathematics is purely metaphorical, it may help explain certain ideas even if we deal with

---

[23]Philip Mirowski, *Against Mechanism* (Totowa, New Jersey: Rowman and Littlefield, 1988), chapter 2.

philosophical ideas, or theories relevant in psychological research. I would like to present a rather interesting example of this kind, in order to further clarify the meaning of the "purely metaphorical use" of analogies, and to show also the limits of this use. This illustration brings forth again a great thinker already mentioned in chapter 5, Nishida Kitaro, the most famous Japanese philosopher of the post-Meiji era. He was the founder of the Kyoto school of philosophy which comprised, among others, Tanabe, Hisamatsu, Ueda Shizuteru and Keiji Nishitani. Daisetz Suzuki (another name already mentioned), who made Zen known to the Western world during the first half of this century, was his best friend. Nishida began his philosophical career with a book published in 1911, *An Inquiry into the Good*: "One had to wait for Nishida for a work that could disprove Nakae Chomin's judgment (in 1900) that there was no philosophy in Japan....Nishida's work is the first to deserve the name of philosophy."[24] Nishida's philosophical quest started with the question "How is the (rational) *understanding* of the pure experience of *satori*, enlightenment, possible?" The Zen believer had—as philosopher—another difficulty: how to single out the *Self* as an independent entity, separated from the surrounding *Wholeness*. The difficult-to-understand (to the Western mind) notion of the all-inclusive "emptiness," *sunyata* or *mu* (in Japanese), does not allow for the objectification of the thinking "I." We find therefore the Zen philosopher (until Nishida, a contradiction in terms!) trying the impossible: that is, to explain by means of concepts borrowed from philosophy, something which seemed to be a priori impossible (the Zen experience). Nishida found that the only way out was to use metaphors and his choice was the mathematical metaphor. Throughout his entire work Nishida used mathematical symbolism; I will exemplify his method by means of an article reproducing in print the content of a public lecture.[25]

The lecture entitled "Coincidentia Oppositorum and Love" ("CO and Love" hereafter) was delivered at the Otani University in Kyoto, in 1919. In the preface to the *Inquiry*, the book mentioned above, Nishida wrote that "an individual exists because there is experience," but throughout this entire book he sounded somewhat Hegelian. He clarified his original ideas in a second book published in 1917, *Intuition and Reflection in the Self-Consciousness*. This was the book in which Nishida began to develop a logical approach to what he defined as the "pure experience." The talk

---

[24]Nakamura Yugiro, quoted by John C. Maraldo in *Japan in Traditional and Postmodern Perspectives* (Albany: State University of New York Press, 1995), p. 228.
[25]This article had been recently published in English translation in the *Eastern Buddhist*, 30, no. 1 (1997).

"CO and Love" was therefore delivered while the author was developing what later was to be known as the "logic of unobjectifiable reality" (like Hegel, Nishida equated logic with metaphysics). And what is more "unobjectifiable" than affectivity? In the Western philosophical tradition, logic and affectivity were—from Socrates to Hegel—in strong opposition. Spinoza's "non ridere, non lugere, neque detestari sed intelligere" (do not laugh, do not lament, do not curse, just do understand) culminated a few centuries later in Hegel's famous statement about the real being rational and the rational only being real. That is where Kierkegaard's revolt against Hegel began, and that is where we find the sources of the later, twentieth-century existentialism (or rather a certain brand of existentialism, that of Shestov and his follower Benjamin Fondane). We are therefore surprised to hear Nishida opening his talk by stating, "I believe (that) logic is linked at its root to human emotion" (see also chapter 5)! To prove this point was the main task Nishida took upon himself in his lecture. His approach anticipates in a way Jasper's method of "formal transcending" in metaphysical thinking. He basically establishes a double identity, one between logic and coincidentia oppositorum (CO) and another between CO and love (which obviously represents affectivity). The link between logic and affectivity immediately follows. Is this procedure convincing? I do not know; I do not want to judge. Here I only want to show how a mathematical metaphor helped Nishida to "demonstrate" the identity between CO an logic. Let us therefore follow this path only.

After a brief presentation of the concept of CO and its evolution from Nicolas Cusanus to Hegel, Nishida dwells mainly on the latter's discussion of the concept. However, I think that Schelling should be more relevant than Hegel when we try to understand Nishida's interpretation of "intuitive knowledge." Indeed, Schelling tried to overcome the great epistemological difficulty left by Kant insofar as the possibility of the knowledge of an Absolute was concerned. For him, the Absolute represented the identity between the Self and everything else external to it. Kant in the *Critique of Judgment* argued against the possibility of an "intellectual intuition"; such an intuition, if related to reason, would be impossible, since rational knowledge requires a necessary distinction between subject and object. Schelling claimed that such an "intellectual intuition" was possible and to prove his point he too used a mathematical analogy. How does a mathematician arrive at the "thought" of the abstract concept of a "triangle"? asked Schelling. He can draw three straight, intersecting lines on the blackboard, determine that the sum of the angles thus formed equals 180 degrees, and call it a "triangle." But how shall we know that *any* such figure, small or large, drawn on the board (on any board), will each have the same property? I must know it through some form of an "intuition" which is not related to the senses (nobody would have to spend his entire life drawing these "triangles," again and again in order to prove the veracity of the above definition). This intellectual (abstract, nonsensorial) intuition is born from the simultaneous perception of the finite, individual triangles drawn on the blackboard, and that of the infinite number of triangles necessarily implied in the concept of "triangle." Intellectual intuition is thus associated with CO, which by one of its definitions is a coincidence of the finite and the infinite.

Nishida wanted to anchor his arguments on more solid grounds, and turned from philosophers (using mathematical analogies) directly to mathematics. He turned to Cantor's ideas about "the nature of infinity." It was a very appropriate choice, since Cantor studied the properties of infinite sets precisely with the idea to clarify the mathematical meaning of "infinity." It is surprising to see Nishida, the Japanese philosopher, using such new and bold ideas that not only passed unnoticed by contemporary philosophers, but were neglected (or even rejected) by mathematicians in Europe. It was not until the turn of the century that a book published in France by L. Couturat, *L'Infini mathématique* (Mathematical Infinity), made extensive use of Cantor's ideas. Very briefly, the key ideas are the following: A set is a collection of objects, books, numbers, etc. In order to compare two sets we need to define a characteristic property of the set(s); Cantor called this property the "power" (*Mächtigkeit*) of the set. If, for instance, we compare set S={1,2,3} with S'={1,2,3,4}, we may say that S is a subset of S' and consequently S has a power which is less than that of S' (assume we call the power of set S, 3 and that of S', 4). The two sets under discussion are finite sets, since the number of elements each set contains is finite. When we go from finite to infinite sets, such as those mentioned by Nishida in his lecture, for instance, the set of natural numbers, N={1,2,...n,...}, the problem of equivalence becomes more complicated: a given set and its subsets may have the same power. For instance, M={2,4,...2n,...}, which is the set of even numbers, is obtained by multiplying by two each natural number in set N. This new set M has the same power as N because of the one-to-one correspondence between the elements of the two sets. At the same time M is clearly a subset of N, because all the numbers in M exist in N, while the opposite is not true. The conclusion is, therefore, that in the case of infinite sets, a set and its subset may have the same power. (The fact that this conclusion is an indirect, but rigorous definition of infinity was recognized both by mathematicians other than Cantor, e.g., Dedekind, and mathematician-philosophers such as Bernard Bolzano.) That is how the metaphor of infinite sets helped Nishida Kitaro to establish an identity between what he called the "self-that-knows" and the "self-that-is-known." This kind of metaphoric use of mathematics may be very persuasive. However, when considered carefully, the argument simply states: My paradox is justified because I found one similar in mathematics! This is the usefulness and this is the limitation of the use of the *mathematical metaphor* across disciplinarian borders.

8

The Issue of "Two Cultures" Revisited

In a lecture delivered more than forty years ago (spring of 1959) as a Rede Lecture at Cambridge University, Sir Charles P. Snow observed that contemporary intellectual life is split into two groups: "literary intellectuals at one pole—at the other, scientists..." (and he singled out as the most representative among them, the physicists). "Between the two, a gulf of mutual incomprehension—sometimes...hostility and dislike, but most of all lack of understanding....Their attitudes are so different that, even on the level of emotion, they can't find much common ground."[1] Since these words were uttered, many things have changed in this world, for the better or for the worse: we entered the era of computers and global networking, life sciences joined natural sciences (physics, chemistry, etc.) in a process that seems to further widen the gap between sciences and humanities, social sciences tried to find their place along, across, or inside the abyss of the divide between the two. Politically, the face of the globe changed, the demography has been radically altered, we are in a new ecological situation; intellectually, we tend to infer from all these changes a transition from a modernity rooted in the Renaissance and the Enlightenment to a postmodernity stemming from complexity and a loss of faith in all the Absolutes. In this radically new situation, does it still make sense to talk about a conflict between two cultures? In his introduction to the most recent edition of the essay under discussion, Stefan Collini points out C.P. Snow's contribution in the following three directions: "He had launched a phrase perhaps even a concept...he had formulated a question...which any reflective observer of modern societies needs to address, and he had started a controversy which was to be remarkable for its scope, its duration, and, at least at times, its

---

[1]Charles P. Snow, *The Two Cultures* (Cambridge: Cambridge University Press, 1993), p. 4.

intensity."[2] Indeed, why "two cultures," why not three, or more? By definition our "postmodernist world" is a many-cultured one as we shall see further; I will argue however in the following that the division into two cultures, in the sense defined by C.P. Snow, conserves its meaning even in a postmodern frame of reference.

Western (Judeo-Christian) culture is based upon a dualistic mind. It begins with the distinction between the *I*, the reflecting ego and the *non-I*, which is the surrounding world. As a result, there is man and God, the immanent and the transcendent, the appearance and the Idea, the subjective and the objective. After the GN revolution, knowledge was divided along the same lines. The culture of the subjective was more and more separated from that of objective knowledge. Since I want to avoid a lengthy discussion about the role of this dualism in Western thought (interesting in itself and not at all besides the point in our context, but it seems that entire libraries have been written already on the subject), let us just observe first, that as we discover more and more about the world surrounding us—at a microscopic as well as on the cosmic scale—we face more questions and new dilemmas. Secondly, as it was often pointed out, our questions belong to one of the following two (again dualism!) categories: they are either "why" or "how" questions. In other words, questions related to the *meaning* of things and questions related to the *functioning* or *relationships* between things. If a falling rock hits me, I may try to understand *how* it happened, and through a series of reasoning arrive at the concept of gravity and Newton's laws, or I may ask *why* it happened to me and why today. Did I commit any wrongdoing? Did I tell a lie or did I hurt a friend? The first attitude would be called scientific. The second might belong to psychology, to theology, or to ethics (the explanation requires a moral judgment, implies a finality or a teleological bent). Let us say then, that whenever we relate to a problem in a way that requires the finding of a *quantitative* and *verifiable* relationship, which seems necessary without having been supposed a priori to be such, we are in the realm of scientific culture.[3] It has been pointed out, in particular by the school of British analytical philosophy, that in this realm the "why" questions, the search for "meaning" (implying a value judgment), have no right to existence. But these questions are asked all the time; they simply exist. At times they

---

[2]Ibid., p. vii.
[3]There is no need to plunge, in the present context, into the interesting but difficult discussion concerning the nature of the law, reproducibility, possibility to infirm, etc.; from Hume to Karl Popper there is an entire literature on the subject. For good and selective readings on these subjects, I recommend beginning with an anthology such as *The Routledge Companion to the History of Modern Science* (London and New York: Routledge, 1996).

even overwhelm us. It is strange but the more we know (scientifically), the more these questions surface. As we marvel at the confirmations and reconfirmations of our abstract models of thinking, we cannot prevent doubts from creeping in. Does God play dice? as Einstein wondered, are we really the result of mere "chance and necessity" as Jacques Monod claimed? With all the science we possess, we cannot get rid of the anxieties rooted in human affectivity. Carl Jung told us that we need the myths. The Romanian philosopher I mentioned in the first part of this book, Lucian Blaga, built an impressive philosophical system based on the idea that thinking human beings *need* mystery: we always act in a world in which faced with our questions (and answers), the horizon of the mystery recedes permanently without ever disappearing. An all-present, all-permeating *mythical culture* is with us, or more accurately, perhaps, within us. If so, there will always be *at least* "two cultures" at work in any modern or postmodern society. We have to face now the question, must they be mutually exclusive?

Why are the "two cultures" separated? Must they be *necessarily* separated? Newton was a deeply religious person and an...alchemist. Goethe, the greatest German poet, is known as the author of a *Treatise on Colors*. James Clarck Maxwell, the founder of modern electromagnetism, was giving lectures to audiences of philosophers in Cambridge. In our century we find many examples of scientists who pondered on the deeper meaning of their findings and of philosophers who tried to understand the foundations of science. Is the problem posed so simply by C.P. Snow, a problem of "perception," of frame of reference, a typical example of biased cultural analysis or a much deeper one, a true incompatibility, a situation of *necessary mutual exclusion*? More importantly, is the problem as defined by its author still relevant? In view of the turmoil created very recently by what certain authors called "the Sokal hoax" (and which I shall refer rather to as the "Sokal incident" in the discussion following in the next chapter), it seems that we still face the problem of the conflict between "literary intellectuals" and scientists at the level of the dialogue across cultural divides. Cultural areas are constituted of clusters or domains of intellectual activity, subdivided in turn into disciplines. Thus, science could be divided, roughly, into life sciences and natural sciences, which in turn can be split again into such disciplines as physics, chemistry and biology, genetics, etc., respectively. *Is the nature of the individual discipline or the mere existence of disciplines the decisive factor in the dialogue—or the lack of it—between cultures?*

C.P. Snow was worried by the conflict *between* cultures, but what about the fight *within* cultures? I would like to dwell for a moment on this topic, in order to offer a glimpse into what could be defined as an "intracultural conflict"; obviously this type of conflict is as real within the "hard sciences," as it is among "literary intellectuals." But while we do not seem surprised by the second (in humanities "truth" is much more difficult to "prove," etc.), we wonder about what could fuel a conflict inside a domain solidly anchored in the hard ground of logical thinking. As an illustration, let us consider the specific example of the debate which took place in physics around the notions of *determinism* and *predictability*. Since the beginning days of quantum mechanics, between the two world wars, the puzzle of the "uncertainty principle," the wave-particle dualism, Einstein's dictum that "God doesn't play dice" and the interpretation of quantum mechanics by the Copenhagen school (which means mainly Niels Bohr) led to a fiery dispute between the advocates of the "deterministic" vs. the "probabilistic" approach. Hume and Kant were revisited, and everybody involved in the discussion (dispute, quarrel?) seemed to struggle with the following question: Since our knowledge of the microscopic (quantum) system is necessarily limited, must we describe it in probabilistic terms (an epistemological problem) or is the reality of the system itself random and, as a result, (ontologically) undeterministic? A contemporary physicist defines the terms of the dispute simply thus: "In a nutshell, *determinism* has to do with how Nature behaves, and *predictability* is related to what the human beings are able to observe, analyze, and compute."[4] Ontology (or, what "the nature of nature" is) is clearly separated from epistemology (our ability to observe, analyze, and explain). But Werner Heisenberg, one of the founding fathers of quantum mechanics, wrote that the probability function "which represents the experimental situation at the time of the measurement...can be connected with reality only if one essential condition is fulfilled: if a new measurement is made to determine a certain property of the system."[5] The probability function describing the quantum mechanical system is "partly a fact and partly our knowledge of the fact," added Heisenberg.[6] Here, ontology and epistemology are inextricably mixed. This situation has created quite a bit of confusion among the scientists themselves; even though since Francis Bacon science was supposed to answer only the "how" questions (in opposition to the "why" ones, left to metaphysics), twentieth-century physics has developed under the shadow of strange questions, such as, is an electron

---

[4]Jean Bricmont in Paul R. Gross, Norman Levitt and Michael W. Lewis, eds., *The Flight from Science and Reason* (Baltimore: Johns Hopkins University Press, 1996), p. 133.
[5]Werner Heisenberg, *Physics and Philosophy* (New York: Harcourt, Brace, 1958), pp. 47-48.
[6]Ibid.

a particle or a wave? and what happens to an electron (or a nuclear or an atomic system) in between two observations?

In the beginning the discussions were intense, but constructive; the disputes Einstein had with the representatives of the Copenhagen school are well documented. His attempts to show that quantum mechanics is probabilistic only because it is an incomplete theory are well summarized in the paper describing the so-called Einstein-Podolsky-Rosen (EPR) paradox. The EPR story has been extensively discussed among physicists (the EPR paper, published in 1935 in the prestigious *Physical Review*, is one of the most often quoted papers written in this century), and Bell's theorem some thirty years later came as a crucial contribution to the debate triggered by this paper.[7] Less discussed until recently was the lifetime effort of another bright mind of the century, David Bohm, to build a deterministic quantum mechanical theory. Like everybody else, young Bohm was puzzled by the above-mentioned questions; but the dialectical-materialistic (Marxist) point of view he adopted as a young student "naturally" inclined him toward a deterministic worldview.[8] His idea of "hidden variables" was anchored in the ideas of Boltzmann and the observation of Brownian motion; Bohm used an explanation similar to that given to explain the random movement of the pollen grains floating in water to explain the apparent randomness observed in the behavior of quantum particles. Electrons or atoms are "moved" between two observations by much smaller, invisible particles, which continuously impact on them. If a special field governing the hidden variables, the "quantum potential," is added, the electrons could be shown to move on actual deterministic trajectories. (Bohm worked out a quantum mechanics based on these principles, which has been refined over time and vindicated later by the observation of the "nonlocality" of the quantum systems.)

It is important to note that the discussion very briefly sketched above continues till today. No less important is it to remark that this is a discussion localized—historically—at the very root of modern physics, but it is by no means the most arduous and the most relevant for contemporary physics. It would be far beyond the scope of this book to

---

[7]The EPR paper is described in almost any popularized account of the philosophical foundations of quantum mechanics; even in books having strong postmodernist bias, for instance, John Gillott and Manjit Kumar, *Science and the Retreat from Reason* (New York: Monthly Review Press, 1997). The physics student should read the original papers; the general reader can begin with the above-mentioned *Routledge Companion* (n. 3).

[8]For the general reader, see David Peat, *Infinite Potential* (Reading: Helix Books, 1997); again, physics students should try to read Bohm's original book, *Quantum Theory*.

enter into these discussions. Instead, I would like to move a step "aside" and present a somewhat similar discussion involving a mathematician, René Thom, and representatives of what he himself calls "the popular French epistemology." The debate is not unlike the previously described one, among physicists; this is a debate about "chance" and "necessity." The thinkers Thom takes issue with are, among others, Jacques Monod and Ilya Prigogine, well-known (Nobel laureates) scientists in their fields of research (which are biology and chemistry respectively, and not epistemology!), Edgar Morin (a sociologist) and Henri Atlan (a biophysicist), both very well known in the French cultural realm and beyond. Thom attacks "the fascination with randomness" of these authors and bluntly states that "in a large measure it proceeds from a certain deliberate mental confusion, *excusable in writers of literary formation*, but difficult to pardon in men of science who in principle have been trained in the rigors of scientific rationality."[9] After asking the question "is the word subject to a rigorous determinism or is there a 'chance' that is irreducible to any description?" Thom goes back to the languages or formalisms by which the phenomena which are the objects of scientific investigation are described. For him there are two types of descriptions: one carried in the natural language (NL) and the other, that of mathematical formalism (M). M has the advantage of predictability. Now, "it can happen," writes Thom, "that a natural system admits a precise mathematical description...; then the sub-objects of the system, which in this formalism can be described linguistically, are objects of a simple form. They are geometric objects for this formalism. If one follows the temporal evolution described by mathematical formalism, two cases are possible. In the first case, this evolution preserves the linguistically describable 'geometric' objects...one can speak then of systems having controllable evolution." But there is another possibility, adds Thom, when "the linguistic formalism loses all efficacy for describing these forms; the only entities which remain accessible to description in the asymptotic state of the system are defined by *mean values* of invariant measures extended over *the whole space*." And, concludes Thom, "in order to preserve a certain control of the system, one must pass from a detailed—microscopic—description of the system, to a *sketchy, global description of a statistical character*."[10] Therefore, it is *the description* which is "chancy," has the appearance of randomness, not the reality described. The world is deterministic, orderly, it is just that our ability to describe it is limited. In the process of description, we introduce disorder,

---

[9] All the articles discussed in the following have been published in a special issue of the journal *Substance* 12, no. 3 (1983).
[10] Ibid., p.14; my emphasis.

randomness, and chance. As we have seen above, Bricmont the physicist says the same thing as Thom the mathematician.

But there are other physicists, mathematicians, and biologists who would oppose these points of view; what Thom rejected was the attempt to answer the fundamental question science is confronted with, "how can the *describable* emerge from the *indescribable*?" with the sophism—as he calls it—of "order through noise." And on goes the debate with Prigogine and Monod and Morin and Atlan and many others. Morin, for instance, after observing that Thom's postulate is ultimately that "the entire plane of reality is algorithmizable," asks "whether there do not exist, in the real universe, things which are non-algorithmizable, non-reducible, non-unifiable; that is things which are uncertain, unpredictable, random, disordered, antagonistic?"[11] Henri Atlan points out that a position of dogmatic and exclusive determinism such as that adopted by Thom leads to the denial of the possibility of the *new*: "The new can emerge only to the precise extent that it could not be predicted."[12] He brings also an interesting example to illustrate the "relativity" of the deterministic and random characters of an observation. Consider, says Atlan, the fabrication by a computer of random sequences using deterministic algorithms. "The random or deterministic character evidently depends upon where the observer is situated in making the judgment: deterministic if one observes the algorithm at the level of its functioning; random if one observes the produced sequence and applies tests of autocorrelation and predictability designed to discover whether it has an order."[13] Prigogine, in his response to Thom, begins by stating that he found in his argumentations "peremptory assertions which can only be explained by the emotional attitude of the author" (which proves that when it comes to sensitive topics, even scientists may tend to replace rational argument with affective outcries!). In essence, Prigogine reverses Thom's question, by stating that "at stake therefore, is the genesis of the 'describable' from the 'indescribable' or, to avoid any misunderstanding, of macroscopic organization from the fluctuating."[14] He points out the distinction between his and von Foerster's view on emergence: while the latter when speaking of "order from noise" is referring to a phenomenon of organization in the domain of equilibrium, Prigogine is talking of macroscopic organization from fluctuations in systems far from equilibrium. And so on and so forth.

---

[11]Ibid., p. 24.
[12]Ibid., p. 44.
[13]Ibid., p. 45.
[14]Ibid., p. 38.

At this point we do not want to pick up on Thom's remark above about "the mental confusion, excusable in writers of literary formation." The next chapter is dedicated to this issue. We may however conclude that even within domains situated safely on the one side of the divide, we may discover "a gulf of mutual incomprehension." It will not be surprising therefore to find incomprehension between cultures situated far apart. For one, their methodologies in approaching and defining a problem are different. In the *scientific culture*, we look for verifiable, quantitative relationships, and these require mathematics, namely, mathematical relationships. As we have seen in the first part of the book, a certain kind of science was practiced in the ancient Greek and other ancient Eastern civilizations. Verifiability was accomplished in Egyptian and Chaldean astronomical observations. Quantitative relationships were sought and obtained by Archimedes. But as we have seen, science became science in the modern sense not only when it accepted the experiment as its main criterion for knowledge, but when it linked the mathematical operation to any and every method of research. Contemporary philosophy of science has tried to analyze and understand the meaning of such basic concepts as that of "experiment" and "experimental evidence" or the meaning of the "mathematization of the research," etc. Those who want to learn more on this subject must read the works of Reichenbach, Schlipp, Popper, Kuhn, and Lakatos, who all made important contributions in these areas. The question of the scientific method was extensively studied. Moreover, the questions relative to the ways to distinguish between scientific theories, or how to compare alternative explanatory theories and decide which one is the correct one (which in turn leads to the question concerning the "truth content" of a given theory), have been passionately disputed among the above authors. But in the context of our discussion, I must point out one aspect of these works pertinent to the question regarding the origins of another battle announced—true, in an indirect way by C.P. Snow—that between the representatives of the postmodernist paradigm and the world of so-called hard sciences. In all fairness I must say that the roots of at least some of the postmodernist criticisms vis-à-vis sciences are to be found in the "internal" criticism arising from the philosophers who have taken a positivist approach to science. Popper and Kuhn have both attacked the notion of the strict separation between experiment and theory. Following different arguments, both concluded that any experiment is affected by an underlying theoretical conception of the scientist who performs it.[15] Later, another important personality in this

---

[15]Most of these arguments are found in Thomas S. Kuhn, *The Structure of the Scientific Revolutions* (Chicago: Chicago University Press, 1970); and Karl R.

field, Paul Feyerabend, added another blow when he claimed in his famous book *Against Method* that one cannot and should not look for "scientific method" simply because there is no such thing.[16] Moreover, he made the argument that the scientific endeavor is just a cultural tradition, among others. Now, if there is no method in scientific research, if inconsistent theories may bring progress by becoming consistent at later times, if one can force certain ideologically motivated ideas upon the science and get away with it because the theory was thus improved, it is no wonder that Feyerabend, before Lyotard or Foucault, and from a very different perspective, reached the conclusion that science can be viewed merely as an ideology among many other ideologies.

The *humanistic sciences* (in the very large sense used here, including everything related to the human individual and human society, from psychology to sociology, history, and political science) do not necessarily require quantitative relationships, nor can they always claim verifiability. Singular, nonreproducible occurrences are acceptable as objects of theoretical inquiry. In spite of this, reason and logical reasoning are used here as much as in scientific endeavor, but imagination and intuition have perhaps a larger impact on the research. It is interesting to note a difference between the two cultures on a "dynamic scale," too: their internal characteristic time scales (that is, the typical times for a significant event to take place) are very different. In particular, this difference becomes obvious in our postmodernist times: science produces new science at a rate incomparable with the one at which (significant) humanistic culture is produced. Of course, in the latter one has to somehow "average" various domains: the literary and even religious "isms" seem to change at a very fast pace today. Still, our "mentality," our cultural biases (used here as a measure of the "humanistic thinking" reflected in our mental processes) change slowly.

One might suspect that the confrontation between the two cultures started much before our times. Perhaps it was always present to some degree. Many believe, as Collini pointed out in his introduction to *The Two Cultures*, that the "concern about the divide between the 'two cultures' essentially dates from the nineteenth century." My argument will be that the conflict predates the modern era; it is more important, however, to realize that with the birth of disciplinarian thinking, the illusion of the European Enlightenment concerning the possibilities opened to the human mind became a dangerous intellectual trap. Humanistics had to become "scientific" by following the example set by

---

Popper, *The Logic of Scientific Discovery* (London: Hutchinson, 1968); and *Objective Knowledge* (Oxford: Oxford University Press, 1972).
[16]Paul K. Feyerabend, *Against Method* (London: New Left Books, 1975).

natural philosophy. In any event, the questions related to the history of the conflict between the two cultures and its very nature are difficult. Regardless of the specific aspects, to even begin such a discussion we need to have some way to estimate the degree of antagonism between two opposite views, a definition of a critical threshold at which the antagonism becomes a "confrontation," etc. In a general way, we may claim that as long as the human individual accepted a "mythical" worldview (as defined in the first part of the book) as prevalent, there was no "confrontation." Even if Aristotle was as close as anyone could have been to being a scientist in the ancient world, he muddled many things just because of this prevalence of the mythical over the scientific, in his own ways of thinking. (Even though in some cases this turned out to be beneficial: declaring matter a "potential" thing, just because it was supposed to have been created by the gods ex nihilo, he became in a way a prophet announcing modern physics. For some strange reason this point is rarely made; Leucippus and Democritos alone are considered the announcers of the atomic theory.)

We could, without much intellectual effort, trace our "problem" to the dispute between the followers of Plato and the skeptics in ancient Greece. We should remember that *skeptein* means "to observe." Believe what you observe, the skeptics seem to say, and do not trust the existence of abstract and out-of-this-world ideas. But we could try to find the roots of our problem in the confrontation between Taoists and realists in ancient China as well. I believe however that the source of the clash between the two cultures is to be found where the source of science as we define it now is, namely, in the dispute between the *nominalists* and the *realists* in medieval Europe. This dispute was at the origin of the Galilean-Newtonian scientific revolution, and as a result, it is also at the root of the "problem of the two cultures." It has often been remarked that the "experimental attitude" of the seventeenth century (Francis Bacon and the members of the British Royal Society) had its roots in the *nominalist* way of thinking, with its emphasis on the *individual* and the *concrete* as the only *reality* in space and in time. The *generic concepts*, of Aristotelian origin, were rejected by the nominalists as *flatus vocis* (breezes of words, unreal shadows of real things), and replaced with the request for unbiased, quantitative experimentation. It is also true that the rethinking of Aristotle on the *realist* side was very important, and again Francis Bacon (who in his *Novum Organum* offered an indirect criticism of the Aristotelian logic) should be mentioned.

From this great debate, which continued several centuries in Europe, Copernicus, Galileo, and Newton were born, and from them modern and contemporary science. In fact, till the beginning of the nineteenth century, scientists were called "natural philosophers" in Europe. It seems therefore that philosophy should belong to the "scientific culture." The careful reader has probably noticed already that until now I prudently avoided situating philosophy in our discussion. Where does philosophy belong? Greek philosophy, born in the pursuit of wisdom (*philo-sophia*), clearly belonged to the "humanistic culture." But Greek philosophy accepted only knowledge obtained through reason. At about the same time (or maybe even somewhat earlier), the same happened in India and China. And if it is true that science did not stem from philosophy in the Far East, as it did in the West, it is also true that there is still an important "Eastern component" in medieval European philosophy. That because medieval philosophy in Europe—that from which the Galilean-Newtonian science was born—was in fact the product of a fusion between Greek philosophy and the Judeo-Christian religion. But the Christian religion was (to some extent, at least) a reformulation of Judaism using Eastern religious and philosophical concepts. This is how, in an indirect way, the East came to play a role in the development of modern "Western science!"

The medieval European philosophers were faced with a great difficulty: how to reconcile the gains of the rational Greek philosophy, which led to the idea of the autonomy of reason, with the belief in the main tenets of Christianity? Aristotle had discovered the existence of truths independent of God's will; he named them *veritates emencipatae a Deo*. On the other hand, one had to believe in the miracles performed by Jesus, in the singularity of his appearance, in the triple nature of the monotheistic divinity, etc. The God of the New Testament, even if He was not an "angry God" anymore, remained a very much "involved" God very much like the God of the Old Testament. The questions concerning the autonomy of reason, the nature of divine law, the reciprocal relation between faith and reason fueled a centuries-long battle. The problem persisted till the dawn of modern times: Leibnitz still spoke of the eternal truths that are in the mind of God independently of His will. Only, Nietzsche's proclamation of "God's death" in the nineteenth century put an end to this centuries-old dilemma.

Philosophers contemporary with the birth of the "scientific culture" were in many cases scientists too; Descartes and Pascal are such examples. Those who were not, were very close to the "scientific mind"; Spinoza with his already mentioned *non ridere* is perhaps the best illustration in that respect. But since they all believed in God (even if in the case of Spinoza it was a pantheistic god), one cannot consider them as belonging exclusively to the "scientific culture." Or should we? By asking this question, we point out another difficulty *within* our problem: does belonging to one of the two "cultures" require a total and exclusive identification with its ways of thinking and its practices? Would a religious scientist belong to the "scientific" or the "humanistic" culture?

As we have seen already, Descartes exemplified this "internal" conflict: his approach was as scientific as it could have been. There was an object for knowledge, the *res extensa*, independent of the thinking mind. The external world had its own laws, and it was not necessary for these laws to have any teleological character. On the other hand, Descartes, by proving the existence of God, implicitly declared his system teleological! Another interesting case is that of Pascal, a deeply religious philosopher-scientist. As he reflected upon the nature of man, seemingly the only being who possessed this magical ability to understand, Pascal came to his famous conclusion: "Man is but a reed, the weakest one in all nature. It is quite unnecessary for the whole universe to be mobilized to crush him; a vapor or a drop of water is quite enough to kill him...even if the universe were to crush him, man will still be more noble than what kills him because he knows he dies, and...the universe knows nothing."[17] What Pascal says is quite clear: man's most precious and noble ability is his ability to think. Through rational thinking man discovers the secrets of the world, that is, the natural laws. But after having said this, Pascal the scientist surprises us when he writes: "When I consider how short a time my life lasts...and how small is the space I occupy or even that I can see, lost as I am in the infinite immensity of spaces which I do not know and which do not know me...I am appalled....The eternal silence of these infinite spaces frighten me."[18] More than three hundred years later, another French man equipped with all the knowledge and the tools of modern science, Jacques Monod (whom we mentioned already), explained to us "scientifically" the significance of Pascal's words: the fear of solitude and the need for a complete and binding explanation are inborn in man! If "fear of solitude" and "need for explanation" are inborn in us indeed, we shall never be able to separate the "two cultures" in ourselves! You shall find your "humanistic culture" within your scientific one, Pascal seems to have said; quite a paradoxical conclusion. It may seem therefore that the real problem of the "two cultures" is not at all related to the existence of two distinct entities, a "scientific" and a "humanistic" culture. Nor would the conflict between them be determined by the fact that an individual happens to belong to this or that culture. The conflict seems to be of a purely subjective nature, seems to be related rather to an inner need to make (or to refuse to make) an individual choice related to the meaning

---

[17]In the original volume of the *Pensées*, this quote is to be found in section 6, p. 347. Blaise Pascal, *Pensées* (Paris: Nelson, Editeurs, n.d.), p. 194.
[18]Ibid.

of the intellectual endeavor. But how do we confer meaning, and on what grounds shall we make our choices? We seem to turn in closed loops. In order to try to further clarify these questions we shall continue, and follow further the idea of the "conflict."

9

Disciplinarity, Interdisciplinarity, and the Sokal "Incident"

Alan Sokal, a professor of physics at New York University, published in the spring/summer 1996 issue of the cultural-studies journal *Social Text* an article entitled "Transgressing the Boundaries: Toward a Transformative Hermeneutics of Quantum Gravity."[1] Since then, this apparently innocent parody has become known as "the Sokal hoax." Not willing to exacerbate a dispute already very heated, I prefer to refer to this event as the Sokal "incident." (Some view the incident as an attempt to introduce a wooden horse into the Troy of postmodernism.) In a nutshell, the article was a fake, a parody; it was a nonsensical text, built though upon a wealth of quotations almost all genuine. And that was exactly the point Sokal was trying to make: the dialogue between the "two cultures," or between any cultures, even the dialogue within a given culture, suggested Sokal, may become meaningless when we abandon the fundamental condition underlying any dialogue: a reciprocal consensus and a common understanding of the basic concepts used by those involved in it. In an afterword to "Transgressing the Boundaries," published by Sokal in *Dissent* (fall 1996 issue), he explained the technique he used: real quotes from famous texts written by famous scientists (and not only scientists) were connected through a multitude of astutely built truths, half-truths, quarter-truths, and falsehoods. For the writer (and his colleagues) "Transgressing the Boundaries" was a nonsensical text. For some "literary intellectuals" it seemed to represent a coherent discourse, it had meaning. How could such a thing be possible? Does that mean that in the present climate, the price we have to pay for a dialogue is having one partner go deaf (which

---

[1] The article is reprinted as an appendix in Alan Sokal and Jean Bricmont, *Fashionable Nonsense* (New York: Picador USA, 1998).

is to say, intellectually numb)? Or is this a demonstration of the fact that the dialogue had become impossible? Which would be equivalent with saying that the dialogue would be possible only if it held Alice's wonderland?

In hindsight, it seems to me that the Sokal "incident" was bound to happen; in fact it was announced, like a major earthquake, by quite a few predecessors. One of them was the collective volume *The Flight from Science and Reason* published in 1996 by the New York Academy of Sciences (quoted already in the previous chapter). A cursory glance at the titles included in this volume gives a feeling for the bitterness and the anger of some of the authors: "In Praise of Intolerance and Charlatanism in the Academia," "Quantum Philosophy: The Flight from Reason in Science, Physics and Common Nonsense," "Science of Chaos or Chaos in Science," etc. In these articles the reader finds at times sober arguments, at times passionate diatribes, all of which reflect deep antagonisms between the "two cultures" as well as a discomfort with the idea of interdisciplinarity. The reader has the feeling that the fight is no longer carried on in the street, a fight between the learned and the ignorant impostors: no, the sacred places of learning, the cathedrals of thought and thinking have been penetrated by the rot. "The academic enemies of the very *raison d'être* of the university can be grouped into two bands: the anti-scientists, who often call themselves 'postmodernists' and the pseudoscientists."[2] And Mario Bunge continues: "Existentialism is a jumble of nonsense, falsity, and platitude," and in support of his assertion he brings a few quotes from Heidegger. Then, he takes issue with Marcuse and Foucault who claimed that "the search for scientific knowledge would be just a disguise for the struggle for power," and with Sandra Harding for "calling Newton's laws of motion, 'Newton's rape manual'" (the rape victim would be Mother Nature, which of course is feminine);[3] the new-style sociologists of science regard science, writes Bunge, "as an ideology, a power tool, an inscription making device with no legitimate claim to universal truth."[4]

Two of the editors of the above-mentioned book, Paul Gross and Norman Levitt, published soon after a work entitled *Higher Superstition*.[5] This book is written as a defense of science against the corrosive deconstructionist acid of so-called postmodernism, which is nothing else in the opinion of the authors than a masque behind which a neo-Marxist

---

[2]*The Flight from Science and Reason* (see full reference in the previous chapter, n. 4), p. 97.
[3]Ibid., p. 101.
[4]Ibid., p. 105.
[5]Paul R. Gross and Norman Levitt, *Higher Superstition* (Baltimore and London: Johns Hopkins University Press, 1998).

academic left hides itself. "To put it bluntly the academic left hates science," write the authors already in their introductory chapter, and continue: "They accuse science itself of a reactionary obscurantism, and they revile it as an ideological prop of the present order, which many of them despise and hope to abolish."[6] We are a long way from the timid attitude of the "literary intellectuals" toward science and scientists. Sir Charles Snow's prophesy implied in the observation made forty years ago that "the separation between the scientists and non-scientists is much less bridgeable among the young"[7] seems to have become a harsh reality, with the addition that the nonscientists passed to the counteroffensive during the seventies and the eighties and the scientists, feeling menaced, counterattacked a decade later.

Therefore, we do not face any longer a benign academic quarrel or a misunderstanding between two groups of cultivated people, arising from the split of the intellectual life of Western society as Snow presented it. Instead, we face a dangerous polarization which can lead to a situation in which the two camps will cease to communicate at all, or still worse, will declare crusades and holy wars against each other. Honestly, today the feeling is that an outright war has broken out between the "two cultures." If the Sokal "incident" and the storm it provoked represented the first salvos of that "war," the heavy shelling began after the publication by Sokal and his Belgian colleague Jean Bricmont (theoretical physicist at Louvain University) of the book first entitled *Impostures intellectuelles*.[8] The book, subtitled in English *Postmodern Intellectuals' Abuse of Science*, attempts a more extensive discussion of the problems posed by the original Sokal article, as well as an extension of the discussion to issues triggered by the article published in *Social Text*. *Fashionable Nonsense* transgresses the problem of the fight between "two cultures" as announced by C.P. Snow. While still addressing a conflictual situation in the realm of culture, it raises a fundamental (and possibly new) question: On which ground is this war fought? Who is the trespasser: the scientist who is trying to use (or some would say, to impose) his methods in fields other than his own, or the humanist who finds hidden (whether social or metaphysical) meanings in the content and the practice of science? I believe that the positive aspect of this negative battle is the implicit acknowledgment, by the two camps, of a common ground; it becomes more and more obvious today that the interpenetration of the intellectual disciplines under the pressure of

---

[6]Ibid., pp. 2, 3.
[7]*The Two Cultures* (see n. 1 in the previous chapter), p. 17.
[8](Paris: Odile Jacob, 1997); the book first appeared in French and was recently published in English translation as *Fashionable Nonsense* (see n. 1, above).

increasingly complex surroundings—material as well as cultural or spiritual—tends to create a unified "battlefield" for the two (or more) cultures confronting each other.

However, before continuing further in this direction, let us pause for a brief moment to consider this very puzzling (and at the same time, very pertinent) question: How was the "hoax" possible? It is obvious that the text was not considered a parody, let alone a trap, by its first readers (the editors, I suppose). While the title might have sounded a bit suspicious ("transformative hermeneutics"?), the introductory paragraphs seemed to have a quite convincing tone. Perhaps not for the ears of a "practicing" scientist (say, a physicist), but for somebody involved with the poststructuralist-postmodernist sociology of science they must have made sense. It is all right to claim, in such a frame of reference, that the hegemony of the Enlightenment "project," which affirmed that "there exists an external world, whose properties are independent of any individual human being" and "these properties are encoded in 'eternal' physical laws,"[9] is challenged today by many. It shows a sign of scientific distinction and intellectual honesty from the side of a physicist to accept the veracity of criticism coming from such remote quarters as those of history and philosophy of science or feminist and poststructuralist criticism. The reviewers must have been charmed by this noble attitude of the physicist who, maybe somewhat embarrassed but devoid of any selfishness, accepts that scientific knowledge is far from being objective. But at this point already, only one page into the text, there are two things which should have alerted an attentive reader: the words *reality* and *knowledge* were written between inverted commas. In addition, a sentence such as the following is too "strong" for a physicist involved in active research: "physical 'reality,' no less than social 'reality' is at bottom a social and a linguistic construct."[10] True, Feyerabend, as we have seen, was not far from saying just that; but he was not an active physicist. A physicist who would come to the conclusion that science is a social or a linguistic construct would probably abandon physics and switch to social or linguistic studies. And that because he would try to find there the solid ground, the "true reality." This process is unavoidable; we have seen in the previous chapters that the *disciplinarian thinking* which made the GN scientific revolution possible had become in time the epistemological ground for all disciplines—including those belonging to the humanities—as they strived to become more and more "scientific." In the process, the basic concepts derived were such that they not only had to be quantifiable, and thus used always in conjunction

---

[9]Sokal and Bricmont, p. 213.
[10]Ibid.

with mathematics, but they had to fit a *reality* upon which the rigors of "verifiability" and "reproducibility" were imposed. For instance, a *mathematical pendulum* is a pendulum having a point mass attached to a string and which oscillates with small amplitude in a frictionless movement. The laws of motion of this abstract device can be found with such accuracy, following Newtonian mechanics, that modern time-measuring devices could be built based on this "theory." This successful coupling between mathematizable (phantasmic) concepts (point mass, frictionless movement) and the reality described by them becomes possible (and has been proven possible in an endless number of cases) only if one element is fixed, external, and independent of any subjective judgment. The requirements of reproducibility and verifiability impose this fixed, objective character on reality. That is why it would be difficult for an active physicist to accept that "his" reality can be a social or linguistic construct.

From this moment on, the signs that something was wrong with Sokal's article began to accumulate at an increasing pace, and in a less and less subtle way: it was claimed that "the space-time manifold ceases to exist as an objective physical reality," that "geometry becomes relational and contextual."[11] Such statements might sound plausible indeed to someone who wants to hear that physical reality is subjective and meaning is contextual. Certainly the straightforward (that is, the simplistic, out of their physical context) reading of the quotations from famous twentieth-century scientists, such as Heisenberg and Bohr, veiled somewhat the author's intentions: Niels Bohr writes that "a complete elucidation of one and the same object may require diverse points of view which defy a unique description." This sounds very much like one of the basic tenets of postmodernist theory. Except that Bohr talks about an electron and the "diverse points of view" he refers to are imposed by the necessity to describe a quantum object, by its nature microscopic, in terms of a discourse (concepts, laws) developed for a macroscopic world. The point made by Bohr is not easy to understand sometimes even among physicists.[12] But even if Sokal's discourse is still veiled, there are already at this stage some uncomfortable hints in the references quoted; thus, for instance, in note 19 we find a reference to Bataille's general economy. Then we read, "For further discussion of Bataille's physics, see...." Which Bataille? The French philosopher and writer? Did he write about physics? Was there an important physicist with this name? the

---

[11] Ibid., p. 214.
[12] Witness to that is a long discussion, spread over several issues of a journal published by the American Physical Society, triggered by Mara Beller's article: "The Sokal Hoax: At Whom Are We Laughing?" *Physics Today*, 51, no. 9 (1998):29.

reviewer should have asked. The suspicion should have been even further raised by the next reference, in which a strange argument about "the deconstruction [which] attempts to elaborate a discourse that says neither 'either/or,' nor 'both/and'..." is connected with...the "complementary principle" of Niels Bohr! Against this background comes the mention of Paul McCarthy's "thought-provoking analysis" which must have triggered all the alarms: "This study traces the nature and the consequences of the circulation of desire in a postmodern order of things...."[13] After that, the "blows" come one after another: "In mathematical terms, Derrida's observation relates to the invariance of the Einstein field equation...under non-linear space-time diffeomorfisms..."; "the *pi* of Euclid and the *G* of Newton, formerly thought to be constant and universal are now perceived in their ineluctable historicity...";[14] "as Lacan suspected, there is an intimate connection between the external structure of the physical world and its inner psychological representation *qua* knot theory."[15]

It is quite understandable that a sociologist of science will view science in ways different from those of the practicing scientist himself. We have already seen a few examples. The question which will arise in this case is, to what extent his/her utterances about science can be correct. We have discussed in chapter 7, the "Schrödinger case"; a physicist explained his ways of understanding biology. Evelyn Fox Keller, a feminist theorist with a background in both biology and physics, addresses in a series of articles[16] the same problem: How do physicists act on the "foreign" ground of biology? This question is at the very heart of our attempt here, the attempt to understand interdisciplinarity. But Fox Keller sees from the very beginning the story of the rise of molecular biology as a reenactment of the drama "between visibility and invisibility, between light and dark...between female procreativity and male productivity."[17] She agrees that the physicists I mentioned, Schrödinger, Delbrück, and Szilard, had an important role to play; but instead of focusing on the concrete contribution each of them brought to biology, she transforms the whole thing into an "attitudinal problem." She quotes Szilard as saying that it was "not any skills acquired in physics, but rather an attitude" which was responsible for

---

[13] Sokal quotes a few lines from this article in his "Comments to the Parody," published as Appendix B in the book. See Sokal and Bricmont, p. 261.
[14] Sokal and Bricmont, p. 224.
[15] Ibid., p. 230.
[16] E. Fox Keller, "From Secrets of Life to Secrets of Death and Language" and "Ideology in Evolutionary Theory," both printed in *Three Cultures* (The Hague: Universitaire Pers Rotterdam, 1989).
[17] Ibid., p. 5.

their successful impact on biology, "the conviction which few biologists had at the time that mysteries can be solved."[18] Thus the interdisciplinarian questions disappear; the whole thing becomes a "story of cognitive politics," in the words of Fox Keller. It is possible that physicists brought into biology an infusion of optimism and it might be that they influenced the attitude of the biologists toward their own field of research. But were Watson and Crick influenced more by these "attitudinal" factors than by the thorough and sound analysis of Schrödinger? Certainly not, as both Watson and Crick witnessed; in Stephen Jay Gould's contribution to the collective volume already quoted, *What is Life? The Next Fifty Years*, one reads: "Jim Watson credits Schrödinger's book as a decisive influence in persuading him to study the structure of the gene."[19] Gould himself states clearly that "it is undeniable that Erwin Schrödinger's *What Is Life?* ranks among the most important books in 20th century biology."[20] It is not always clear why, and different authors have found different reasons for this influence; whatever the reasons though, we find that among scientists they always had to do with the *content* of the interdisciplinarian effort and not with its *motivation*. We see therefore that the Sokal article raises a very basic question concerning the possibility of the dialogue between the "two cultures," between disciplines. But in view of the above example, we begin to understand the angle of his attack: if in order to prove something you have to have a "scheme," a preconceived idea about the importance of a certain factor in the explanation of the facts, briefly, if the motivation is more important than the content, he will play by this rule. Therefore he entirely scrambled the content, but made sure that the rhetoric was kept steady. Granted, for a person coming from the side of humanities, the terminology and the meaning of certain assertions was increasingly difficult. What to do faced with an impossible scientific jargon? The most logical thing would have been to consult a scientist. That might have been difficult, since scientists are not very forthcoming in discussing the epistemologic and ontologic grounds of their work. There are a few who did (and do) it, but in general, unless someone is close to retirement or has received the Nobel prize, the active scientist will be reluctant to consider the "philosophical" implications of his work. Many will consider it a waste of time, some will be afraid of being compromised in the eyes of their peers. But if asked to collaborate with a colleague from across the divide to disentangle a problem—such as the meaning of an article like that written by Sokal—he would probably

---

[18]Ibid, p. 6.
[19]See reference described in n. 9, chap. 7; p. 25.
[20]Ibid.

collaborate. As I said, there is no doubt that after the first page, the physicist would have sensed something strange. The real question is however this: If Sokal had eliminated all the incorrect utterances in the realm of physics, would the physicist have been able to help out his colleague? As stated already, a physicist would not accept the idea that the object he studies is a mere "linguistic construct"; he may find some difficulty with accepting the social motivations (or implications even) of his work. But what would he do with the quotation above concerning Lacan and the inner representation we have of the structure of the physical world? What does a physicist know about Lacan? True, Sokal added a clue, which would have made plain to the physicist the hidden intention of the text: he continued the above quote with the incredible, "this hypothesis has recently been confirmed by Witten's derivation of knot invariants...." In its own intricate context, the work of Witten is certainly not fabulation, but his work does not bear any relationship with Lacanian topology whatsoever! Now the physicist knows that the whole thing is a joke, or a hoax. What can he say to his friend the editor of *Social Text*? Is there any common ground on which the representatives of the "two cultures" can meet? Does an interdisciplinarity defined in the "static" sense as the common ground where disciplines meet really exist? I believe that in the last analysis, the conflictual aspect of the Sokal enterprise is less important. The question we started out with, how was the hoax possible? is much less significant than why was such a thing possible? Is there such a degree of incomprehension between the representatives of the "two cultures," between disciplines, to the point that we cannot distinguish any longer between the *real* and the *parody of the real*?

Sokal and Bricmont in writing their book adopted a somewhat militant attitude: they defined their enterprise as a "critique of the admittedly nebulous Zeitgeist that we have called 'postmodernism.'" Many of the postmodernist writings are permeated by such "abuses": among them, the use of scientific theories without understanding them, indiscriminately importing concepts from one culture into the other, displaying fake erudition, and manipulating meaningless sentences. In the view of the authors, the book was a follow-up to the questions triggered by the article. Bricmont himself was annoyed by abuses inside his own field of research: endless discussions around the "philosophy of quantum mechanics" (he wrote a long article against the "philosophy of quantum mechanics," quoted already), around "chance and necessity," "indeterminacy and complementarity," around the famous Einsteinian question does God play dice? and more recently, chaos theory. But as long as the discussion is kept within a given discipline, that is, it is carried on among active researchers in that given domain, the debate may be heated but it will always make sense. On the other hand, any time interdisciplinarity, genuine or not, is attempted, the debate quickly degenerates (with, so far, very few exceptions) and evolves toward a meaningless confrontation. When Lacan fails in his use of topology, when Latour, Baudrillard, Deleuze, and Guattari abuse scientific concepts and construct images and theories which do not make any sense to a scientist (as Sokal and Bricmont have shown), do they really fail in their enterprise, or are we the scientists those who fail to understand them? Is there any way to distinguish between these two situations?

In his book *Science: The Glorious Entertainment*, Jacques Barzun makes a very important point: "Science belongs to mankind. *We* made it—we the merchants, craftsmen, theologians, scholars, metaphysicians, and manual laborers."[21] Science is undoubtedly flourishing, he adds, man is *not* flourishing. The rich Western societies, as well as the advanced communist countries (in spite of their propaganda claiming the opposite), lived with this uneasy feeling ever since the Second World War. Science pushed modern technologies (even if it is true that technology is not really the offspring of science), science made possible unprecedented kinds of warfare and limitless mass destruction, science penetrated *culture* to the point of taking it over. It had become inevitable that "literary intellectuals," writers, sociologists, historians, philosophers, would address these problems. It is legitimate to feel that consumer society and cultural mass production have something to do with science. The moral dilemmas raised by the menace of mass destruction or impending ecological catastrophes set us on a frantic search for the roots of our problems. The estrangement, the anxiety felt by intellectuals confronted with a world which seemed more and more incomprehensible, more detached, more mechanical, and as a result, capable of degenerating into monstrous and inhuman social structures, was traced back to its supposed source in science and the menacing "scientific culture." For the most part, the scientists were quiet. Others, watching things from outside the realm of science, tried to interpret these phenomena. From Max Weber to the Frankfurt school, from Walter Benjamin to Daniel Bell, from Bataille to Baudrillard, there were many voices of "literary intellectuals" who tried to find out what role science plays in the predicament of contemporary mankind. What kind of tools were they supposed to use in this endeavor? Those of science, the subject of their investigation, or their own tools, philosophical, socioeconomic, psychological? Was it not unavoidable that the concepts, the intellectual

---

[21]Jacques Barzun, *Science: The Glorious Entertainment* (New York: Harper and Row, 1964), p. 283.

constructs, the imagery used would mix? That the sociological or ideological interpretation of the meaning and even the content of the scientific output would be judged on grounds foreign to science? Of course, all this was to be expected, and indeed, it happened. But once it happened (and once triggered, the process evolved on a large scale), the products of these analyses were found to be strange creatures: illegitimate monsters for the scientists or menacing extraterrestrials for the creators themselves.

The questions these intercultural or *interdisciplinary* endeavors give rise to are of course very complex. After having read Sokal and Bricmont, we are bound to repeat the questions asked already at the end of the first part of this book. We know what it means to act *within* a discipline, but how to proceed when from inside one given discipline we want to make a statement concerning another discipline? Can we carry our tools across the boundaries? Do we have to modify them as we cross the boundaries? Can the new tools handle the job? Who is going to have the authority to decide whether the mission was accomplished or, on the contrary, it was totally botched? *Scientism* is a term often used to describe the essence of the scientific endeavor. I preferred to use instead a more accurate one, that of *disciplinarian thinking*. It is very important to realize that this disciplinarian thinking has permeated to a large extent the humanities and the literary intellectuals themselves. My argument is that a critique from "outside" is possible only if one would be able to rid himself of the patterns of thought imposed by disciplinarian thinking. The attempt of modern cultural studies (all those names mentioned above, and many more, who contributed to what they—and not only they—would call the "postmodern revolution") to reappraise and reset our ways of thinking failed because this residual of disciplinarian thinking lay in their own ways of thinking. Underneath and behind existentialism (of the Sartrian brand), structuralism, poststructuralism and other isms, under Foucault, and Barthes and Lacan, and Lyotard and Baudrillard and Deleuze and Guattari, we find the traces of the thinkers of the GN revolution, Bacon, Descartes, and Leibnitz, of the French Encyclopedists, of Marx and Freud. Is it then surprising that the scientists reading the output of the "postmodernist thinkers" get upset? That Sokal wanted to make the points mentioned above? Sokal would not have been able to pass off his parody as real, if the discourse, the patterns of thought of those on the two sides of the divide, had not had so many things in common. The postmodernist revolution is not a revolution. It is an old skeleton covered with a new garb. Ultimately, it is not the legitimacy of the critique of the sciences from outside which is fiercely disputed by Sokal, Bricmont, and many others, but the poor intellectual quality of the enterprise. To conclude this chapter, I shall illustrate this point with a few examples.

I mentioned earlier the word *quantofrenia*. It stood, in the context in which it was advanced, for "an exaggerated and ultimately meaningless use of mathematical terms, notations or formulas in areas of research outside that of 'hard sciences'" (defined precisely as those disciplines in which one can efficiently use mathematics). Lacan was an abusive user of mathematics in psychology/psychiatry. In their book, Sokal and Bricmont discuss a few outstanding examples; I have chosen them to serve as illustrations of the main argument, but at the same time, they will serve us in the analysis of the deeper argument that in fact wrong or right, Lacan is still a prisoner of disciplinarian thinking. While he gives legitimacy to the use of metaphor in scientific knowledge (human psychology in this case), he seeks first and foremost the "real." To make his points he uses mathematical terminology; the subject (the mind) contends Lacan, is some kind of a knot into which a complicated code was inscribed. A sphere, the old symbol for totality, does not adequately describe this folded message. One has to make use of more complicated topological structures: "A torus, a Klein bottle, a cross-cut surface, are able to receive such a cut."[22] A "cut," we are led to understand, would somehow be related with a given mental state (or disease): "One can show that a cut on a torus corresponds to the neurotic subject."[23] Is this a metaphor or is each mental state some sort of a real complex topological structure? To the question whether, "this fundamental arithmetic and this topology are not in themselves a myth or at best merely an analogy for an explanation of the life of the mind?" Lacan answers: "This torus really exists and is exactly the structure of the neurotic. It is not an analogon, not even an abstraction...I think it is reality itself." The topological concepts have been made into operational concepts which describe, that is, are in a "one-to-one" correspondence with, an objective reality. This is, as we have seen, pure disciplinarian thinking.

Sometimes however, a metaphor is a just a metaphor, even if it is a mathematical one: "Human life can be defined as calculus in which zero was irrational. This formula is just an image, a mathematical metaphor. When I say 'irrational,' I'm referring not to some unfathomable emotional state but precisely to what is called an imaginary number...[which in spite of being such] must be conserved, along with its full function."[24] Here Lacan says that he is building around a "mathematical metaphor," but makes an elementary mistake: he

---

[22]Sokal and Bricmont, p. 19.
[23]Ibid.
[24]Ibid., p. 25.

confounds "imaginary" with "irrational" numbers. For anybody trained in elementary mathematics, this would be enough to reject any (and all) Lacan's mathematical imagery! What in fact Lacan wanted to express through the "life as a calculus in which zero was irrational" metaphor (zero is dividing the axis of all numbers, it is situated in the middle, at the core, at the center) was his assertion that the core of our lives is irrational. In spite of that, we must not reject this irrational aspect of our lives, exactly as we accept the definition and the use of irrational numbers in mathematics. It is a point which may be debated, but it is a point which has been rather nicely expressed through this—mathematically mistaken—metaphor. Still, he was not given the benefit of the doubt, and his metaphor was lost on Sokal and Bricmont, because of the enormity of the mistake (from a mathematical point of view). Somebody from the field of the humanities may retort to this that the judgment of the scientists is too harsh: ultimately, we can understand what Lacan wants to convey through his metaphor even if he makes the mistake of calling an irrational number an imaginary one. But this is precisely the problem at the core of the dialogue, at the core of the use of mathematics in certain disciplines: *no*, one cannot forgo such a mistake. Mathematics is a rigorous and logical intellectual enterprise. One cannot make any concessions because concession means a breaking of the logic underlying the system; as a result, the system loses its self-consistency, which is the guarantor of the truth contained within it.

One may make another argument also, a more "human" one: he who doesn't pay attention once will be bound to make the same mistake (of confusing things) again, and the second time the "mess" may be even more serious. Unfortunately, Lacan is a perfect example of how true this argument is. At some point he makes the impressive statement, "I demonstrate the strict equivalence between topology and structure." Sokal and Bricmont go a long way (they find the relevant references) to show that Lacan doesn't know what he is talking about. "If this term is understood broadly—that is, as including linguistic and social structures as well as mathematical structures—then it clearly cannot be reduced to the purely mathematical notion of 'topology.' If, on the other hand, one understands 'structure' in its strictly mathematical sense, then one sees easily that topology is one type of structure, but that there exist many others: order structure, group structure, vector-space structure, etc."[25] *Quod erat demonstrandum.*

---

[25]Ibid., p. 22.

10

Is a Dialogue Possible?

The previous two chapters unfolded the story of a contemporary conflict between cultural domains and disciplines which divide and define the totality of human intellectual endeavors. One was told in the frame of modernity, that is, under the assumption of the existence of absolute and objective truths, of the undisputed legitimacy of such concepts as the *immanent* and the *transcendent* (considered as general and not only as theological categories of thought). The other story has been presented in the light of the fragmented and relativized worldview which is currently called postmodernism.[1] (It is interesting to note that in spite of the many French [Foucault, Lyotard, Baudrillard], German [Benjamin, Habermas] and American [too many to risk mentioning only a few] names brought up in the postmodernist context, it was in fact the historian Arnold Toynbee who first introduced—in his vast *Study of History*—the distinction between the modern and the postmodern ages in the historical context.) In both cases however, we found at the core of the dispute the question of communication, the question concerning the possibility of dialogue between different human intellectual activities, the relationship between *disciplines*. If one accepts the legitimacy of absolute frames of reference, the question will be how to redescribe facts and relationships when moving from one frame to the other. In a way this is the question of the transfer between *Naturwissenschaften* and *Geisteswissenschaften*, as defined by Dilthey, for instance. If, on the other hand, every problem (or "narrative" in postmodernist parlance) is just a description carrying with it its specific frame of reference and all frames

---

[1]There are many books introducing the subject; to begin, one can either read works of those who forged the concept, for instance, Jean-Francois Lyotard, *Le Postmoderne expliqué aux enfants* (Paris: Editions Galilée, 1988) or introductory guides such as Madan Sarup, *Post-Structuralism and Postmodernism* (Athens: University of Georgia Press, 1993).

of reference are equally legitimate, the dialogue seems to be forbidden in principle. It simply disappears, all the cultures becoming one—and thus the dialogue between disciplines (cultures) becomes in fact impossible. Things are not as simple however, and in this last chapter I would like to present and briefly discuss a few attempts toward a dialogue, within both paradigms. By its very nature, the presentation will be fragmentary. Moreover, in the present context such a presentation is also incomplete: a whole book can be written around this subject alone (and in fact many books have been written on several of the topics only briefly mentioned here). Another difficulty stems from the fact that the attempts to bridge (or create) gaps between cultures (whether two or many), or between disciplines, came at different times in different cultures. We can think of the Encyclopedists in France, the post-Newtonians, the Romantics and the Victorians in England, the classical period and the *Aufklärung* in Germany, for instance.

Much has been written about the affinities and the reciprocal rejections between the representative ideas of the classical and the Romantic periods. The times immediately following the GN revolution seemed to have been permeated by a "scientific spirit," followed by a strong reaction to it in the eighteenth century. The nineteenth century seems to swing back and adopt again a positive attitude toward science, but the picture is more "fragmented," it appears as a puzzle composed of many pieces, each having a different color. As we approach the twentieth century, we distinguish a systematic split in the intercultural attitudes: on one side we observe a trend which follows the Romantic movement and tends to reject the "tyranny of reason." This movement had more of a religious-philosophical bent at its beginnings; nonetheless, it tended to create a polarization between the humanistic and the scientific domains. It was the rejection of Hegelianism by Kierkegaard, Nietzsche's revolt, and the penetration of their ideas into literature (sometime in indirect ways, for instance, in the works of Dostoevsky), which paved the road to the twentieth-century existentialism of Shestov, the great deconstructionist of rational thinking. (Shestov's existentialism was of a very different brand than that of Sartre or Heidegger, of Camus or Gabriel Marcel.) After the First World War, Marxism in its various versions (from the simplistic dialectical-materialism of the Leninist brand to the sophisticated one practiced by the members of the Frankfurt school, or by Lukacs and Gramsci, and later, by Leszek Kolakowsky or Althusser) seemed to be the only philosophical counterweight to these emerging trends in humanities. Of course there were Weber and Wittgenstein, Bergson and Husserl, but what was left of them after the Second World War? The real battle was fought between a more and more refined Marxism covered with opaque veils to the point that in France it was sometimes very difficult to recognized it as such, and an existentialism descending from Heidegger and Sartre. In England, the "analytic philosophy" seemed to talk only to itself (and a few followers abroad). All this happened while natural science was literally exploding. The understanding of the basic laws of thermodynamics, optics, and mechanics in the nineteenth century, followed by the discovery of the quantum world and the theory of relativity at the beginning of the twentieth century, led the Western world from the heat engine (the times of Marx) to the A-bomb (the time of Sartre) within a hundred years. As the crisis of rationality seemed to deepen in the area of the humanities— and this includes at least some parts of the social sciences, such as politics and economics to some extent—it was triumphant rationality which seemed to create a technology without (apparent) limits. The irrational sometimes touched the rational, for instance, in Nazi Germany people experienced their co-existence, and in real life, the experience was if not always destructive, often unpleasant. In reality, the coexistence was unacceptable. If Kafka was a literary value, a Kafkaesque world became synonymous with nightmare. Still, as in every conflictual situation, behind the battlefields there are always people who continue their peaceful activities unperturbed. T.H Huxley in Victorian England battled Matthew Arnold; the first represented science, the second was the literary intellectual. His descendent Aldous Huxley, the writer, wrote a book entitled *Literature and Science*. In 1880, T.H. Huxley was inviting those pursuing a humanistic education to study sciences, so that their minds would become clearer and their thinking more purposeful. Science is good for people and for the nation was the implication. Almost seventy years later, a distinguished professor of physics at Cambridge, Sir Lawrence Bragg, was encouraging science undergraduates to study poetry and literature because as new scientific knowledge accumulates it "may only too easily be buried in scientific journals until with the lapse of time it can no longer be of interest or influence the progress of the science. It is important to present new knowledge in a form in which it can be assimilated...and this presentation is an art akin to poetry and literature."[2]

Let us turn back in time and analyze in more detail a few specific attitudes. The Newtonian breakthrough left a trail of optimism among literary people. James Thomson, born in 1700, who was once "the poetic equivalent of the Gideon Bible; his poems were to be found in every inn

---

[2]In the foreword to Thomas R. Henn's book, *The Apple and the Spectroscope: Lectures on Poetry Designed for Science Students at Cambridge* (London: Methuen, 1951).

and cottage in the land,"³ was one of them: "While thus laborious crowds/Ply the rough oar, Philosophy directs/The ruling helm." Here we have to read "natural philosophy" as "Newtonian science," of course. To what extent this is a correct assumption we learn from reading his 209-line elegy *To the Memory of Sir Isaac Newton*, published in 1727, the very year of Newton's death. There was no doubt in the poet's mind that as the great man "quit this earth to mingle with the stars," the muses were "astonished into silence." And in spite of the enormous (intellectual) difficulty, the poet aspires "in Nature's general symphony to join." That Nature which "stood all subdued by him [i.e., Newton], and open laid/Her every latent glory to his view." Thomson was not alone in his enthusiasm for natural philosophy; there were other contemporary poets, such as John Hughes and Richard Glover, who described in superlative words Newton's accomplishments.⁴ Before them, Dryden already requested that "a man should be learned in several sciences and should have a reasonable, philosophical and in some measure a mathematical head, to be a complete and excellent poet" (in *Notes and Observations on the Empress of Morocco*). I cannot help wondering, however, if in this new world dominated by a new way of thinking (disciplinarian thinking) and by the effects of the Puritan rebellion, the poets did not adopt the pragmatical "if you cannot fight them, join them" attitude. The pressure was certainly great: in his *History of the Royal Society of London*, Thomas Sprat was quite harsh and outspoken when demanding that "*eloquence* ought to be banish'd out of all *civil Societies*, as a thing fatal to Peace and good Manners."⁵ What one would have called the "literary intellectuals" of the day (the "Wits" and the "Scholars," as Sprat calls them) were "in open defiance against *Reason*; professing, not to hold much correspondence with that; but with its Slaves, the *Passions*."⁶ And on he goes, to accuse these practitioners of the "easie vanity of *fine Speaking*," of a "vicious abundance of *Phrase*, this trick of *Metaphors*, this volubility of *Tongue*...."⁷ To these, he opposes the practitioners of the natural philosophy (scientists, we would call them today): "They have therefore been most rigorous in putting in execution, the only Remedy, that can be found for this *extravagance*: and that has

---

³Michael Schmidt, *Lives of the Poets* (New York: Alfred A. Knopf, 1999), p. 294.
⁴A very interesting source to be consulted on this subject is Mark Greenberg's article in the volume *Literature and Science*, ed. Stuart Peterfreund (Boston: Northeastern University Press, 1990).
⁵I kept the original spelling, as printed in Thomas Sprat, *The History*, ed. J.I. Cope and H.W. Jones (St. Louis, Missouri: Washington University Studies, 1958), p. 111.
⁶Ibid., p. 112.
⁷Ibid.

Is a Dialogue Possible?

been, a constant resolution, to reject all the amplifications, digressions, and swellings of style....They have exacted from all their members, a close, naked, natural way of speaking; positive expressions, clear senses, a native easiness; *bringing all things as near the Mathematical plainness as they can.*"[8] The "Wits" and the "Scholars" had not been under such pressure since the times of Plato! Moreover, we observe that an idea which will have a significant specific weight in the future argument between the two cultures is beginning to surface during the first part of the eighteenth century: it is that of the historical character of the two cultures. Science is the intellectual endeavor of the future, humanities (again, in the sense given to the term in the context of this discussion) belong to the past. The "spirit of the Royal Society" will be represented in France by Montesquieu and Buffon. And again, we hear distant echoes of the dispute Plato had in ancient times with Homer. The impact of this new way of thinking was so deep that more than a hundred years later, Wordsworth, presenting his "experiments" in the *Preface to Lyrical Ballads*, would write that he intended "to ascertain, how far...that sort of pleasure and that *quantity* of pleasure may be imparted, which a poet may *rationally* endeavor to impart" (my emphasis).

But there were dissenting voices too. By the time William Blake appeared on the scene, the stage was set for confrontation. What is interesting is that in Blake we can find arguments which could be developed in opposite directions, insofar as the conflict between the two cultures is concerned. For the conflict was already there; it suffices to remember his terrible statement so often quoted: "Art is the Tree of Life...Science is the Tree of Death." In the same direction goes his remark—so different from the above quote from Sprat—"God forbid that Truth should be Confined to Mathematical Demonstration!"[9] But William Blake was more than a poet who rejected on Romantic grounds the—intellectually and socially—more and more menacing science. His thinking was founded upon several postulates incompatible with those upon which the natural philosophy, that is the science of his day, was based. Indeed, in the same notes to Reynolds' discourses (written in 1808) we read: "Reason...is not the Same it shall be when we know More."[10] Twenty years earlier, he was saying the same exact thing in the *Didactic and Symbolical Works*: Reason, or "the ratio of all we have already known, is not the same that it shall be when we know more."[11] In plain

---

[8]Ibid., p. 113; my emphasis.
[9]All the quotations from Blake are from *Poetry and Prose of William Blake*, ed. Geoffrey Keynes (London: Nonesuch Press, 1927), p. 1009.
[10]Ibid.
[11]Ibid., p. 148.

words, this is an open warning: Careful gentlemen, Newton's laws may not be as absolute as you think; as we learn more, we may find out that they may not apply to planets as well as to atoms.

But there was more than a "relativization of rational thinking" in Blake. It seems to me that a new ontology can be found in his writings. The poem entitled "The Human Abstract" (from the *Songs of Experience*) ends with the statement that in spite of the suprahuman ("the Gods of the Earth and See") efforts to find "thro' Nature" the Tree of Knowledge, "...their search was all in vain: There grows one in the Human Brain." Blake acknowledges that "the true method of knowledge is experiment"[12] and this is achieved by our organs of perception. But, he adds, man "perceives more than sense can discover." How? Through *poetic genius*. Poetic genius enables man to see the Infinite in all things, and only those individuals who possess this intellectual ability might hope to reach the transcendental, to establish communication with God. "He who sees the Infinite in all things, sees God. He who sees the Ratio only, sees himself only."[13] Newton's science, that is, the "philosophy of the five senses," binds the human beings to earth, restricts them to the condition of "slaves to the eternal elements." In *The Song of Los* (1795), we read:

> Thus the terrible race of Los & Enitharmon gave
> Laws & Religions to the sons of Har, binding them more
> And more to Earth, closing and restraining,
> Till a Philosophy of Five Senses was complete.
> Urizen wept and gave it into the hands of Newton & Locke.[14]

The new ontology I was alluding to above stems from this mixing of epistemology with ontology: the essence of the object of knowledge depends on an inner faculty of the searching individual. As knowledge increases, this faculty develops further and, in turn, creates new knowledge to be acquired. That is why Blake will rhetorically ask: "What is General nature? is there Such a Thing? what is General Knowledge? is there such a Thing?" and will conclude, "Strictly Speaking all Knowledge is Particular."[15] It is not my intention to pursue here the questions related to knowledge, truth, and ultimate reality in Blake any further; it has been observed that due to the volume of his work and the opacity of his intellectual discourse, almost any philosophy can be extracted from his writings. The temptation to study his gnosticism or, at the opposite extreme, his atheism is great (Giovani Papini saw in Blake a

---

[12]Ibid.
[13]Ibid.
[14]Ibid., p. 274.
[15]Ibid., p. 989.

mystic who in his relentless search for God—not unlike Meister Eckardt—brought Him so close to man to the point that God becomes a creation of Man). I will only remark that the way he "unfolds" truth reminds one of Heidegger; his blurring of the frontier between epistemology and ontology reminds us of Nishida. And perhaps an even more thought of provoking idea is that William Blake was the prophet of the transition from modernity to postmodernism some two hundred years before it happened.

When in 1821, Percy Bysshe Shelley in his *Defense of Poetry* came to answer Thomas Love Peacock's criticism of "poetic knowledge," as expressed in the "Four Ages of Poetry," both stood therefore on broad and solid shoulders. In Peacock's criticism (even though his essay was considered only a "half-serious essay"; the author was a mediocre poet who, at some point, exchanged poetry writing for a job with East India Company) we recognize the distant, but firm voices of Sprat and the members of the Royal Society and their followers: "A poet in our times is a semi-barbarian in a civilized community. He lives in the days that are past. His ideas, thoughts, feelings, associations, are all with barbarous manners, obsolete customs, and exploded superstitions. The march of his intellect is like that of a crab, backward. The brighter the light diffused around him by the progress of reason, the thicker is the darkness of antiquated barbarism, in which he buries himself like a mole...."[16] The virulence of the attack is astonishing, even by today's standards. (In passing, I would remark that Peacock's poetry sounds indeed like that of somebody implementing—or submitting—to the ideas expressed in his own essay. Here is an example: "The poor man's sins are glaring/In the face of ghostly warning? He is caught in the fact/Of an overt act—/Buying greens on Sunday morning.") The historical character of the two cultures, which I alluded to above, becomes one of the basic arguments in Peacock's essay, which begins with the words: "Poetry, like the world, may be said to have four ages." There are "poetical times" and the beginning of the nineteenth century was an "unpoetical time." The good poems have (already) been written and "there are more good poems already existing than are sufficient to employ that portion of life which any mere reader...should devout to them." The products of the contemporary "unpoetic times" are mere "artificial reconstructions of a few morbid ascetics" who produce "promiscuous rubbish!"[17] In addition, by its nature "poetry is not one of these arts, which like

---

[16]"Four Ages," in *Memoirs of Shelley and Other Essays and Reviews*, ed. H. Mills (New York: New York University Press, 1970), p. 129.
[17]Ibid., p. 130.

painting, require repetition and multiplication."[18] Poetry is dead, and there is nothing one can do about it. It seems to me that here too—as paradoxical as it may seem—we can distinguish an idea originating in Blake (and this is just another illustration of the paradoxical nature of Blake's work). Time is cyclic; anything begins with a soul permeating matter, but when the time comes and the energy has been spent, the age is over and a new age must begin.

Shelley in his response begins by setting a hierarchy: there are "two classes of mental action," reason and imagination, and "Reason is to Imagination as the instrument to the agent, as the body to the spirit, as the *shadow* to the *substance.*"[19] And to dissipate any possible doubt, he adds immediately: "Poetry, in a general sense, may be defined to be 'the expression of the imagination': and poetry is connate with the origin of man."[20] It is interesting to observe that Shelley spends only a brief part of his essay on the discussion of "poetry in its elements and principles." Very quickly he moves on to the main argument in his defense of poetry: the effect poetry has upon society. "Poetry"—argues Shelley—"strengthens that faculty which is the organ of the moral nature of man."[21] A world which tends to "resign the civic crown to *reasoners* and *mechanists*" (my emphasis), a society which considers that reason is more useful than imagination, will end up in a situation where "the rich have become richer, and the poor have become poorer; and the vessel of the state is driven between the Scylla and Charybdis of anarchy and despotism."[22] The salvation could come only from poets and their poetry: "Poets are the...trumpets which sing to battle...the influence which is moved not, but moves. Poets are the unacknowledged legislators of the World," concludes Shelley.[23]

Goethe's approach to the question about the relationship between the two cultures was quite different. Maybe because he was among the few who did not discuss the problem from a well-defined vantage point. He embodied in one person both the scientist and the literary intellectual. While there is no doubt that he fitted the description Shelley gave of the poet, the question regarding his ways in science is more difficult. Was Johann Wolfgang von Goethe a "real" scientist, a scientist in the sense defined by the GN science? Since a detailed discussion of the origins and the essence of the GN science has been undertaken already in

---

[18]Ibid.
[19]*Shelley's Poetry and Prose,* selected and edited by Donald H. Reiman (New York and London: W.W. Norton, 1977), p. 480; my emphasis.
[20]Ibid.
[21]Ibid., p. 488.
[22]Ibid., p. 501.
[23]Ibid., p. 508.

the first part of this work, I will to limit the discussion here to the following, more restricted question: Did Goethe, who was involved in both science and poetry, find himself caught in a conflict between the two tendencies of his mind? For him, the practice of science was synonymous with the search for the manifestation of law and order in natural phenomena. But Goethe possessed too much "Poetic Genius" to seek only simple relationships between objectively defined concepts. Like Blake, he believed that "Knowledge is Particular," that the person who seeks truth has to establish an intimate contact with the object of his research. Novalis, another great poet, wrote a short essay on Goethe in which he expressed this idea in a very suggestive way: "Nature and insight into nature come into being at the same time."[24] Nature can be compared with antiquity, says Novalis; they are both external to the observer, both are independent realities open to observation. "Nature is nothing other than living antiquity," writes Novalis, and defines a very postmodern view of science when, continuing the nature-antiquity metaphor, he adds: "For one is greatly in error if one believes that antiquities exist. Antiquity is only now coming into being. It grows under the eyes and the soul of the artist. The remains of ancient times are only the specific stimuli for the formation of antiquity. Antiquity is not made with hands. The spirit produces it through the eye...."[25] It is customary to excuse the "naive science" Goethe practiced by making him into a phenomenologist *avant la lettre*. But Goethe was far from Husserl. From the exuberant approach of the young poet, "NATURE! We are encompassed and embraced by her—powerless to withdraw, yet powerless to enter more deeply into her being. Uninvited and unforewarned, we are drown into the cycle of her dance and are swept along until, exhausted, we drop from her arms,"[26] to his later "delicate empiricism," we will always find in Goethe the idea of the "mediated truth," the belief that the researcher and the researched object—whether it is a plant or the nature of light and color—must be intertwined, related in some mysterious way. "The True is God-like; it does not appear unmediated, we must guess it from its manifestations."[27] Perhaps through "elective affinities" with Goethe, the other poet, Novalis, gave us the most accurate rendering of Goethe's position concerning the confrontation between the two cultures: "The question of the *reason*, the law of a phenomenon etc. is an abstract one, that is, it is a question

---

[24]Novalis, *Philosophical Writings* (New York: State University of New York Press, 1997), p. 111.
[25]Ibid.
[26]Quoted from *Goethe's Botanical Writings* (Honolulu: University of Hawaii Press, 1952), p. 242.
[27]Ibid.

directed away from the object toward the spirit. It has to do with *appropriation*, assimilation of the object. Through explanation the object ceases to be strange. The spirit strives to absorb the stimulus. What is strange stimulates it. Transformation of what is *strange* into one's own; thus appropriation is the ceaseless business of the spirit. One day there is to be no *stimulus* and nothing *strange* anymore—the spirit is to be strange and stimulating to itself, or will be able to make so intentionally. Now the spirit is spirit out of instinct—a nature spirit. It is to be a rational spirit, to be spirit out of reflection and *art. Nature is to become art and art is to become second nature."*[28] It is a bit difficult to follow Novalis' demonstration of the idea contained in the last sentence of this quote. Rational explanation is an appropriation of the object explained. In the process the external (natural object) ceases to be strange to the internal (spirit, manifested through art). As with Blake, here too epistemology and ontology mix. Also, in the process the spirit triggers the stimulus; at a certain moment, when (ideally) we would know everything and the unknown (the "strange") will be completely absorbed, the stimulus will cease to exist. At that point, the spirit, in a "bootstrapping" process, will become "strange" and will be stimulating to itself. Thus, spirit is *reflecting subject* and *reflected upon object*, at the same time. Art and nature become one, there is no conflict; the activities of one mind within two cultures are indistinguishable.

The above examples more than hint at the complex history of the interactions between the two cultures in time. Of course, the discussion could have been extended to the entire nineteenth century. We would then follow the swings of the pendulum between idealism and positivism, between a new classicism and a new romantic movement, between Darwin and Nietzsche, between Matthew Arnold and T.H. Huxley. Back in time, we could have considered the French Encyclopedists, the discussions between Diderot and D'Alembert, between Voltaire and Rousseau. The pendulum would continue to swing in this century, between surrealism and quantum physics, between existentialism and Marxism. Wolfgang Pauli the physicist joins Jung, while Bergson the philosopher quarrels with Einstein (around the concepts of time and duration). An interesting example of "convergence" between the two cultures is to be found in the person of another poet, Paul Valéry. A representative of the "divergence" is Shestov. In between, most of the prominent representatives of the two cultures in the twentieth century had an ambiguous position.

After the strong rebuttal by F.R. Leavis—*Two Cultures? The Significance of C.P. Snow*, published in *Spectator* (March 9, 1962)—the

---

[28]Novalis, p. 116; my emphasis of last sentence.

Is a Dialogue Possible?

discussion around the problem of "two cultures" faded. (Of course, there were further sporadic discussions and clashes within as well as outside the academic world; a good review can be found in the already mentioned introduction to *The Two Cultures* by Collini.) As we have seen in the last chapters, the dispute between "two cultures" both belonging to one and the same paradigm (that of modernity) had become in time, in the fragmented world of postmodernity, a real battle of all against all. In a way, this interpenetration, this "transgression of boundaries," is good news for interdisciplinarity. On the other hand, we discover how risky this enterprise might be. We have seen in the pages of this book many examples of botched interdisciplinarity. The question of interdisciplinarity is manifold: there is, on one hand, a "factual interdisciplinarity" at work. One cannot prevent sociologists from reflecting upon the way science is produced, one cannot stop scientists from pondering upon the philosophical meaning of their discoveries, or agonizing over the ethical implications of their results. Methods proven to work in one area are tried in other domains of research. Individual and collective interests will bias these interdisciplinary activities. This is as hard a fact as the existence of the person involved in the research and the object of his/her research. Why quarrel then? In earnest, we must recognize that away from the noisy battlegrounds, one can find people in search of new ideas in literary criticism, in hermeneutics, and in general, in the entire field once known as *Kulturphilosophie*. They approach the problems from a completely different angle—by its very nature a nonconflictual one. They try to understand the complex patterns hidden under the surface of the phenomena or the creations (human or natural) they study. At the same time, in their laboratories or in the shadow of their telescopes, scientists think more often than before, not about how to reduce the complicated to the simple, but rather how to understand the structure or the organism, in its complexity. We seem to discern here a common ground, a convergence, which may bring together, *nolens volens*, the representatives of the "two cultures." This new trend toward understanding—in all our intellectual endeavors—the world surrounding us in terms of "levels of complexity" creates a climate favorable to the acknowledgment of a multiplicity of "cultures." But now "cultures" are not defined anymore as domains divided along disciplinarian lines, but as different approaches to a common problem: that of complexity. The effects of this new trend are felt even within the old frames: thus, for instance, somebody referred recently extensively to a "third culture" as being that of the "scientists and other thinkers in the empirical world who, through their work and expository writing, are taking the place of the traditional intellectual in rendering visible the deeper meanings of our lives, redefining who and what we are."[29] It is certainly true that many contemporary scientists are trying to "render visible deeper meanings," whether we talk about complexity, genetics, cosmology, or the "theory of the whole universe." Many more do so than in the past; but do they do it for reasons different from those of Sir Bragg, mentioned earlier? Can today's "literary intellectuals" better understand them? "The non-scientists have a rooted impression that the scientist are shallowly optimistic," wrote C.P. Snow.[30] When we scientists tell people with unshaken authority how the universe came into being, describing in great detail the first three seconds of the universe (as well as the last ones), when we announce that we shall soon finish mapping the human genetic code and as a result, we will understand "it all"—are we not bound to perpetuate this image of the "shallowly optimistic" scientist? "On the other hand," continued Sir Charles, scientists believe that "literary intellectuals are totally lacking in foresight...in a deep sense anti-intellectual, anxious to restrict both art and thought to the existential moment."[31] I could have replaced "existential moment" with "cultural relativity" and we would be back to the uproar caused by the Sokal "incident," discussed in the previous chapter. Whether we accept three cultures or more, nothing will change if the dialogue is to be continued in the old frames. We can imagine though, that from the study of complexity, a new way of thinking can emerge in the long run. Different kinds of concepts, coupled with quantitative as well as qualitative and/or hierarchical relationships would form the conceptual basis of this new way of thinking. These concepts will be used equally well in the study of natural processes as well as in those involving a priori unpredictable changes in the systems studied (emergence of new properties or processes triggered by volitional or affective causes). If the "level of complexity" becomes the defining element of the domain of research, disciplinarity—and as a corollary, interdisciplinarity—as known and practiced today will be overcome. It is intellectually risky, and professionally compromising, to advance such ideas. It is also extremely difficult to attempt even an overview of the ways in which complexity is treated today in various domains. Still, this is the only way we can go in search of a detachment from *disciplinarian thinking*. But if we want to advance the discussion of interdisciplinarity beyond the limits presented in this work, we must attempt it.

---

[29]John Brockman, *The Third Culture* (New York: Simon and Schuster, 1995), p. 17.
[30]*The Two Cultures*, p. 5.
[31]Ibid.

11

Instead of a Conclusion: Fragments for a Book about Interdisciplinarity

Any finished piece of work, be it an article or a book, must have a concluding section or chapter in which the main points are summarized, the central ideas brought forth clearly and distinctly. That is what we teachers always tell our pupils. And we become angry when we discover a work ending abruptly. Students I might have scolded in the past for that reason, as well as the readers of this book, should forgive me for not ending it with a concluding chapter. Since the entire book represents just the beginning of an attempt to position the subject of our inquiry and to hint at some of the central ideas related to it, it is not appropriate to end it with a concluding chapter. Instead, I add to the previous chapters a few scattered thoughts, quotes, and remarks, which represent only a small part of a huge amount of material gathered while preparing this book and written as I was reflecting upon some of its main ideas.

* * * *

Blaga speaks about a "paradisiac" and a "luciferic" thinking. In paradise, Adam had a certain knowledge, that of naming things, of classifying them. He could then learn from this "taxonomic" experience, and even infer laws. This led to Kant. Blaga denied the Kantian *cul-de-sac*. Rational knowledge is limited; but there are the irrational structures of the "luciferic" knowledge, a knowledge which does not dissipate the mystery, but on the contrary creates it in the process of "knowing." "I will not crush the world's corolla of wonders/and I will not kill/with reason/the mysteries I meet along the way...." Blaga was also a great poet.

* * * *

What did Shestov say about knowledge in Paradise? Rational thinking seems to be for Shestov the corollary of the Fall. I find myself trapped again with Shestov.

Blaga: "We are creatures to whom the truth is denied on purpose in order to apply ourselves to creation."

* * * *

Blaga: "The individual knowledge (or the knowledge of the individual) yearns for the truth; it is victim of a deeply engrained fervor anchored in the mere possibility of the 'act of the transcendence.' In spite of that, 'The Great Anonymous' allows this fervor for truth to realize itself only in the negative idea of the mystery (mysterious). Any other type of knowledge is a dissimulation through censorship of the transcendental."

* * * *

Blaga in "The Dogmatic Eon": The myths are distant and separated. Hellenistic Greece begins the process of amalgamation. East and West mix. Myths are compared. A common, underlying *meaning* is found. The meaning changes a vision into an idea; this is the turning point where the myth is converted into an abstract thought. In turn, the abstract ideas are transformed too in a reverse trajectory; the concepts become embodied, they acquire concrete qualities.

* * * *

Blaga points out that while the dogma is a renunciation of rational thinking, it still formulates its content in the realm of the rational.

* * * *

The "essence" of Shestov (in "Athens and Jerusalem"): "*We must send intellectual honesty to the devil, in order to rid ourselves of Kant's postulates and learn to speak with God as our ancestors spoke with Him.*" (p. 378). And also: "Intellectual honesty consists in submitting to reason not externally, through fear, but willingly...what if reason has seized power illegally?"

In the paragraph entitled "The Source of the Metaphysical Truth," Shestov quotes Seneca (whom, he says, as is his custom, always repeats the words of others): "Ipse conditor et creator mundi semel jussit, semper paret" (The Master and Creator of the World himself commanded once and obeys always).

* * * *

We have lost the ability to live with uncertainty: we believe that knowledge keeps us on the track of "being right all the time." If you study, you know. If you know you are right. This is one of the main consequences of *disciplinarian thinking*.

* * * *

Luther: "Whoever wants to be a Christian should tear the eyes out of his reason" and "You must part with reason and not know anything of it and even kill it" and "reason is a whore." Jaspers: "True philosophizing begins only after reason has suffered shipwreck."

* * * *

I found in Noica (another contemporary Romanian philosopher little known in the West) the idea that modern thinking originated in a crisis situated in the epoch preceding it. Bacon, Descartes, and Leibniz were all enemies of the syllogism, says Noica.

Back to Matte Blanco: He has the idea that the *set theory*," matching, or one-to-one correspondence...is at the heart of all thinking." Is he making the same use of it as Nishida Kitaro does? Nishida: "It seems that the creative world, i.e., the world of self-contradictory identity which contains self-negation within itself, possesses a group-theoretical structure!"

* * * *

Vico is the culprit: after Spinoza's *non ridere*, Vico seems to have accredited the "scientific" notion that the "savage" mind evolved from a thinking dominated by feeling, an "imaginative knowledge" to the full conceptual knowledge of the moderns. (see Gustav Jahoda, *Crossroads between Culture and Mind* (Harvester Wheatshif, 1992), p. 26). Is Vico the father of modern "scientism" in humanities?

* * * *

Nishida, Matte Blanco, and Lupasco: All three have responded to the inadequacy of classical logic to handle consciousness (or mind) and try to invent new logics and to use fancy mathematics. Nishida the philosopher came close to cognitive psychology when trying to define *basho* as the locus of his new logic of the predicate. Lupasco tried to arrive at a unified and integrated view of the *Whole:* of material, of life, and of the spiritual. And Matte Blanco, the psychoanalyst, wanted to understand the relationship between conscious and unconscious processes.

* * * *

The next volume should be *A Perplexed among the Guides*; not too bad a title. The insurmountable complexity surrounding us stems not only from the chaotic behavior of the systems which really affect our existence, but also from the impossibility of "closing" them. We live in a world which is unpredictable in all senses. We cannot prevent the man-made catastrophes of the future; we are unable to defend ourselves against major natural catastrophes. "Live and let live" is the only optimistic ideal possible. But is it possible?

* * * *

Why—I was asked in Kyoto—why in order to explain the conflict between "the two cultures" must you go back to the fight between *nominalists* and *realists* in the Middle Ages? Because, I would answer today, the separation between scientific and humanistic culture began when the mythic component was discarded. Monod pointed out (among others) that, "in both primitive and classical cultures, the animist tradition saw knowledge and values stemming from the same source." Sticking to this duality was typical of the realist tradition. The nominalists broke it and opened the door to "experimentalists" like Bacon.

* * * *

Shestov's "deconstruction" of rational thinking is important (at least) for the following reason: we seem to have gone astray in our *conceptualization of experience*. In our divorce from the reality of meaning and its substitution with more and more abstract symbols, or "verbal envelopes, void of all intelligible content" (as put in *The Psychology of Reasoning* by Rignano), we build huge dialectic edifices, pompous systems of thought (or of lack of it; and this is true in science too sometimes!). But today, instead of tearing them down and rebuilding on the ruins from time to time, we grant equal rights to wisdom and to sheer stupidity. Interdisciplinarity should play this role: that of protecting us from the excesses of our own minds. "Real" interdisciplinarity should not really teach how to do things in one discipline using the tools of another, but instead, it should prevent us from becoming stupid and insensitive. Not a very academic endeavor (or statement).

An example: Deconstruction in historical research is apparently motivated by the quest for ways to reject the homogenizing and manipulating narratives of modernity. The ideas of the Enlightenment led to the Holocaust, Lyotard seems to claim; but as Aschheim points out

Instead of a Conclusion: Fragments for a Book about Interdisciplinarity 137

in his *Culture and Catastrophe*, the direct causal link between the two has never been proved. The theory of complex systems insinuates that one shouldn't even try! Moreover, it would indicate that while the above could be a possible outcome, there are other ones, totally different and (almost) equally probable.

* * * *

Bachelard: "the preference of relationship over entity" or "a phenomenon is a tissue of relationships." This is Matte Blanco!

* * * *

From Blaga: "The dogmatism, as we defined it, uses concepts and categories in a special way; that is, as transfigured antinomies."

* * * *

Reading Matte Blanco: Maybe the two logics of symmetrical and a symmetrical thinking have been coexisting in the postperceptual human mind. The one took precedence over the other because it was better adjusted to reality. It is clear though that the "symmetrical thinking" includes the paradox, i.e., the "dogmatic" thinking as defined by Blaga. Blaga also stressed that the dogmatic thinking is logical. Now, what's the difference between them and Lupasco? Lupasco creates a new logic for the asymmetric thinking, which has the advantage of somehow being able to accommodate the affective.

* * * *

Practical interdisciplinarity (of the bad kind perhaps): In connection with Matte Blanco, I had the idea of a *field of the symmetrized singularities*. This would be the realm of the unconscious/affective; its "quanta" are the *singulons*, points of singularity in which the unconscious may find itself. As long as we are *inside* these points, nothing happens; but small infinitesimal movements aside will take us to either positive or negative infinities ($f=const/(y-y')$; at $y=y'$, f becomes infinite). See Matte Blanco/Melanie Klein contradiction. The *asymmetry field* is that of the conscious, of the logical. Its "quanta" are the *concepts* which can be continuously "translated" into objects. Thus, a metaphor belongs to the field of the *singulons* (it cannot be translated into a "real" object). There must be a correspondence between the two fields.

* * * *

From the *Gilgamesh Epic*: Enkidu (Gilgamesh's friend) has been seduced by the courtesan goddess Ishtar and in the process the wild man got "wisdom, broader understanding." Ishtar tells him: "You are wise Enkidu. You are like a God." The idea of the primacy of knowledge over life (tree of knowledge vs. tree of life) comes from Babylon to the West, through the Jews and the Greeks. (And the Egyptians?)

* * * *

Interdisciplinarity has to be replaced with another word. Still, it is not a science but a way out from the labyrinth.

* * * *

There may be a level of reality different from that in which the subject-object separation is ascertained. Nishida calls it "True Reality." This would be the level at which the differentiation subject-object disappears. But this is a *state of mind* while the quantum mechanical world of the duality particle-wave is an ontological reality. (The trouble with Nishida is that he is always oscillating between epistemology and ontology.)

* * * *

I am often asked, why didn't science develop in Japan? but what about, why didn't science develop in Israel? Medieval Jewish thinkers were mostly Aristotelians, but the Kabbala was related to Platonic (or Neoplatonic) thinking. Jews reproduced in their own frame of reference the battle between nominalism and realism. Here is an interesting remark I found in Husik's *History of Medieval Jewish Philosophy*: (In the fourteenth and fifteenth centuries) "philosophy and rationalism begin to be regarded askance, particularly as experience showed that scientific training was not favorable to Jewish steadfastness and loyalty."

* * * *

Important note for the "Interdisciplinarity book": see pp. 70-71 in George Steiner's *Real Presences*, "...the presumption of reciprocity between theory and fact."

* * * *

I can see why some of my colleagues are against interdisciplinarity. Here is a quote from a postmodernist critic: "My second assumption is that *disciplinary boundaries are comforting but illusory props*, necessary as local, social enclaves of organization but dispensable in the larger epistemological scheme of things"!

And another one: "Our century shows a remarkable intellectual unity, a vivacious dialogue between the arts and sciences that can be easily missed by a student working narrowly in a single discipline"!

One more, from the same: "Anthony Wilden, whose own transdisciplinary speculations make him more a critic than an advocate of cybernetics, warns that cybernetic analysis of human behavior and expression such as social organization, economics and psychology results in a reductionism that can only be cured by a cybernetics of cybernetics that will be both *interdisciplinary* and *transdisciplinary*." I am on dangerous grounds!

* * * *

A fine example of interdisciplinarity: Aldous Huxley writes about science. Huxley points out the "nomothetic" character of science in general, but observes that there are sciences which are "ideographic" more than nomothetic. "For science in its totality, the ultimate goal is the creation of a monistic system in which...the world's enormous multiplicity is reduced to something like unity...," he writes in *Literature and Science.*

* * * *

The "new history" (that is, the history we live today, that of complexity) begins with the age of magic. Science, religion, art all try to put order into chaos. In spite of Couliano, magic is living with and by chaos, in chaos. Today, we live in chaos. The magicians were the road openers.

* * * *

The "ahistorical mode" of the nineteenth century, that of the Cartesianization of the social, was prefigured by Grotius! But in this intensely historical time, ahistoricity is a difficult proposition. In any case, I see here a contradiction: in order to make "scientific" the research of the social, one must emphasize the general, the ahistorical. On the other hand, Hegel's influence, direct or by reaction, forces historicity on the social. In addition, there are the anti-Cartesian forces at work since the Romantics and Nietzsche. Impossible to make history into a "science."

* * * *

From a book written by sociologists: Knowledge is "whatever men take to be knowledge...those (collectively endorsed) beliefs which men confidently hold to and live by." One of the authors wrote a book entitled *Wittgenstein: A Social Theory of Knowledge.*

* * * *

From Hobbes' *Leviathan* (Part I): "*Reason* is the *peace*; increase of *Science*, the *way*.... Metaphors and senseless and ambiguous words, are like *ignes fatui*; and reasoning upon them is wandering amongst innumerable absurdities...."

* * * *

Guénon goes beyond the division between the "two cultures" by establishing the division elsewhere: "the traditional doctrines" are neglected completely nowadays and an abyss separates them and "everything that is to-day called by the names of 'science and philosophy'..." (in *The Reign of Quantity*). For him the dispute is not between "two cultures" but between a *culture* identified with "profane instruction" and a *traditional teaching* (the esoteric, the essence of the religious "doctrine").

* * * *

From John Marenbon's *Early Medieval Philosophy*: "In the tenth and eleventh centuries scholars concentrated, though not exclusively, on the metaphysical ideas in the ancient works; the more thorough readers of the twelfth century were preoccupied by their scientific aspect."

Adorno wrote "the whole is untrue," and a commentator added: "Of course, the false whole does exist as the social totality totalized by the means of total, administrative-bureaucratic or even totalitarian practice" (introduction to the chapter "Esthetic Theory and Cultural Criticism" in *The Essential Frankfurt School Reader*). Another example of incomprehensible writing; it is illustrative of my "transformation theory" which explains how incomprehensible German Marxist texts have been transformed into incomprehensible French poststructuralist ones. Nonsense is a universal constant. Like the speed of light, in all frames of reference it is the same.

* * * *

The problem of "interdisciplinary criticism": It is true that while sometimes interdisciplinarity may be beneficial, often it may be

Instead of a Conclusion: Fragments for a Book about Interdisciplinarity

detrimental (see Lurçat on that). Today, when Sokal and Bricmont criticize Lacan or Kristeva, it is legitimate to ask to what extent is this criticism itself legitimate.

* * * *

Each period of "paradoxical thinking" (Christianity, Reformation-belief against belief inside the same religion) generates complexity at a high rate.

* * * *

The question of the relationship between *Rinascimento* and *Rinascita* is essential for my discussion of *disciplinarian thinking*. This way of thinking is a *constant* which unites the two; moreover, it unites them with our times.

* * * *

Disciplinarian thinking originates in Aristotle's *phûsis*: We have been taught to always search for the nature of things. If Plato's philosophy had gained supremacy, maybe thinking wouldn't have gone "disciplinarian."

* * * *

All we can do within the confines of disciplinarian thinking is to transfer "metaphors" and quantitative methods of analysis from discipline to discipline. The metaphor can be used to better explain an idea, or, as in the case of the economics based on the ideas of equilibrium and conservation, the metaphor may serve as the basis for quantitative analysis.

* * * *

Couliano claims that "there is thus a sharp distinction to be drawn between these two great expressions of life: the energetic love, the passive knowledge." That was certainly not true for the "scientific poets" and in particular for Ronsard.

* * * *

Two remarkable stories about John Scottus Eurigena (the Irishman): One is about the conversation with his patron, the king Charles the Bald. "What is there between *sottum* and *Scottum*?" asked the king. "The breadth of the table, Sire" came the answer. It seems that Eurigena was killed by his students who were forced to think too hard by the master, in Malmesbury! On a more serious note, his *Periphyseon* examines the four divisions of Nature: that which creates and is not created (God, theology), that which creates and is created (biology), that which does not create and is created (physics), and that which is not created and does not create (geology). Of course, here "to create" means "to create spirit."

* * * *

Reading Henry H. Bauer, *Scientific Literacy and the Myth of the Scientific Method*: The emphasis is on the "myth of the method," but there are other well-taken points about the division into disciplines, the role of "hard sciences" in other fields, and the social aspects of science and scientific endeavor.

* * * *

The new, "phantasmic concepts," which were such that it was easy to couple them with mathematics, created in turn "cleaner," better focused concepts. Very important point to make in the book. In Pinker's book *How the Mind Works*, a pertinent remark: "the entities now commonly used to explain the mind...intelligence, capacity to form culture...will surely go the way of protoplasm in biology, and of earth, air, fire, etc., in physics...."

* * * *

"Human beings knew about empiricism and skepticism and were capable of logic long before the seventeenth century, and not only in western Europe." The "collective behavior," science as social activity, is claimed by Bauer to be at the origin of modern science. He shows a plot of the evolution of the number of scientific journals in time, which unveils a sharply positively sloped line between 1665 and the present: "...in the seventeenth century the puzzlers began to organize themselves, to specialize, to communicate rapidly with one another, and to act as critics for one another...." Now, the author doesn't deny the cognitive aspects involved in the scientific revolution. His point is that it is the "collectivization" of the scientific effort which caused the breakthrough. But the collective activities existed already in medieval Europe; the only factor added was the speed of the communication. Moreover, one may claim that the need the Church had to supervise the purity of the doctrine and to swiftly react to any heretical tendencies had created the mechanisms for these interactions.

* * * *

In Guénon's *East and West*, there is a chapter on *The Superstition of Science*, in which we read that "in the idea of tradition, all science appeared as an extension of the traditional doctrine itself." That may explain why the Japanese algebra, *wasan*, has never become a "functional" mathematics. That may also be the explanation for the fact that Aristotle's explanations of void and movement remained far remote from reality; that might explain the horror the Greeks had for the "infinite."

* * * *

Guénon and "skewed interdisciplinarity": "Is it not one of the strangest characteristics of modern science that it never knows exactly what the object of its studies really is...?"

* * * *

Aristotle used *general categories*, such as "change," instead of motion. He sought *the nature of the things*. Matter and form were key principles. Lindberg writes: "When an ancient or medieval natural philosopher turned his attention to any area of inquiry, the first thing he wanted to know was: what things (relevant to the inquiry) exist?...Once he settled this question, he could move on to others such as: What is the nature of the things that exist? What kind of existence do they have? How do they change? How do they interact? And how do we know about them?" This last point is as important as the one Blaga makes: Descartes has settled the question of the reliability of our thinking. The division into various domains of intellectual inquiry was not a deep one, a *strongly methodological* one, but a division of convenience. *Change* is a cross-disciplinarian concept, whereas *movement* is associated with a well-defined discipline!

* * * *

Prigogine in *Order out of Chaos* presents Kant, Hegel, and Bergson as attempting to counteract the dominance of the mechanistic-positivist science. Diderot is a precursor in his fight against Newton and Descartes and their *machinisme*. But in fact they were all practitioners of "disciplinarian thinking." The same should be said about Fourier, the father of the new science of complexity. When he establishes the famous law of heat conduction as proportional to the gradient of the temperature, he is creating the adequate concepts and mathematizing them, as everybody.

* * * *

The "phantasmic concepts" could be introduced only after (1) the long intermezzo of the scholastic-abstract thinking and (2) the overcoming of the paradox through its "taming" and rationalization.

* * * *

Heidegger is not saying about science anything really new after Kant and Blaga; the first has defined the "mathematical project" (*Entwurf*) of Heidegger ("upon the basis of the mathematical, the experientia becomes the modern experiment") in the *Critique of Pure Reason*, as follows: "...reason only gains insight into what it produces itself according to its own projects." Blaga talked about the necessity to make the concept mathematizable; all of them talk in fact about "phantasmic" concepts.

* * * *

Why did Stoicism and Neoplatonism lose the battle with the emerging Christianity? Somebody wrote that it was because "their symbols were too abstract and they demanded more maturity and independence of mind than most people possessed."

* * * *

A reversal of positions occurred: The GN revolution stemmed from a nominalist attitude of scientists, but once the disciplinarian thinking was installed, a slide toward realism occurred. In our days, the positions have been reversed: the humanists are the nominalists. As a result they tend to look more at the practical, social implications of *all* things, including intellectual activities. They see that in *arts* the social substratum is essential, so they extrapolate it to sciences too. The trouble is that the analysis doesn't work because of the residuals of *disciplinarian thinking* in the humanities.